Creative Beginnings

An Introduction
to Jazz Improvisation

Scott D. Reeves

University of Southern Maine

PRENTICE HALL   Upper Saddle River, New Jersey 07458

Library of Congress Cataloging-in-Publication Data

Reeves, Scott D.
   Creative beginnings: an introduction to jazz improvisation/
Scott D. Reeves.
     p.   cm.
   Includes index.
   ISBN 0–13–345463–0
   1. Jazz—Instruction and study.   2. Improvisation (Music) 3. Big band
music—Instruction and study.   I. Title.
MT68.R368 1997
781.65′ 136—dc20
                                      96–13933
                                          CIP
                                           MN

Acquisitions editor:	Bud Therien
Editorial/production supervision, interior design:	Jenny Moss
Copy editor:	Carole Crouse
Buyer:	Robert Anderson
Editorial assistant:	Lee Mamunes

This book was set in 10/12 Palatino by Thompson Type and MPT Music
Engraving and was printed and bound by Courier Companies, Inc. The cover
was printed by Courier Companies, Inc.

Epigraph sources:

page 1: Bill Milkowski, "Swing, Soul, Sincerity—A Bobby McFerrin
   Workshop," *Downbeat*, 60, no. 11 (November 1993), 58.

page 19: Nat Hentoff, *Jazz Is* (New York: Limelight Editions, 1992), p. 267.

page 113: Zan Stewart, "The Spirit of Collaboration—Melba Liston & Randy
   Weston," *Downbeat*, 62, no. 2 (February 1995), 24.

page 159: Herb Wong, "Stan Getz," *Jazz Educators Journal*, 24, no. 1 (Fall
   1991), 59.

page 223: Howard Mandel, "Pat Metheny Plays It His Way," *Downbeat*, 62,
   no. 4 (April 1995), 18.

page 277: Kenny Werner, personal conversation with author. Scotch Plains,
   New Jersey, June 1992.

page 306: Fred Shuster, "Risk Your Life for Every Note," *Downbeat*, 62, no. 8
   (August 1994), 19.

© 1997 by Prentice-Hall, Inc.
Simon & Schuster/A Viacom Company
Upper Saddle River, New Jersey 07458

Printed in the United States of America
10 9 8 7 6 5 4 3 2 1

ISBN 0-13-345463-0

Prentice-Hall International (UK) Limited, *London*
Prentice-Hall of Australia Pty. Limited, *Sydney*
Prentice-Hall Canada Inc., *Toronto*
Prentice-Hall Hispanoamericana, S.A., *Mexico*
Prentice-Hall of India Private Limited, *New Delhi*
Prentice-Hall of Japan, Inc., *Tokyo*
Simon & Schuster Asia Pte. Ltd., *Singapore*
Editora Prentice-Hall do Brasil, Ltda., *Rio de Janeiro*

With appreciation to my wife, Janet, for her encouragement, proofreading, and piano voicings; Paul Pitts and other band directors in Maine, Massachusetts, and Vermont for field-testing the manuscript; Bud Therien, Lee Mamunes, Jenny Moss, Carole Crouse, and staff at Prentice Hall; Janet Reeves, Bronek Suchanek, and Les Harris, Jr., for their musical contributions to the companion CD; Jamey Aebersold for the concept of the play-along recording; and Kenny Werner for his continued inspiration.

CONTENTS

CD SELECTIONS

Selections listed are on the CD available from the publisher.

CD Track	Selection	Text Chapter
1	Tuning Notes: B-flat and A Concert	
Warm-Ups:		
2	Rhythm Warm-Ups: Latin Rhythms	3
3	Rhythm Warm-Ups: Swing Rhythms	3
4	Major Scale Warm-Ups	4
5	Mixolydian and Bebop 7th Warm-Ups	5
6	Dorian Scale Warm-Ups/ Blues Scale Warm-Ups	6, 8
7	ii–V–I Progression Warm-Ups/ Diminished Scale Warm-Ups	7, 13
8	Melodic Minor Scale Warm-Ups	10
9	ii$^{\emptyset}$7–V7♭9–i Warm-Ups	11
10	Minor Pentatonic Scale Warm-Ups	12
Improvising on Jazz Compositions:		
11	"Another Spring" (Scott Reeves)	4
12	"Sister Cynda" (Scott Reeves)	5
13	"Eric's Song" (Scott Reeves)	6
14	"The Countess" (Scott Reeves)	7
15	"Eta Carina Blue" (Scott Reeves)	8
16	"Lester Lept Out" (Scott Reeves)	9
17	"Double Entendre" (Scott Reeves)	10
18	"Blue Autumn" (Scott Reeves)	11
19	"El Corazón" (Scott Reeves)	12
20	"Nuthouse" (Scott Reeves)	13

PREFACE

This text grew out of a need for an entry-level companion to my first text for Prentice Hall, *Creative Jazz Improvisation*. Although that book has gained acceptance as a popular text for college-level courses and intermediate-to-advanced students, some of the material proved too difficult for high school groups and students relatively new to the art of jazz improvisation.

Features of This Text

Creative Beginnings utilizes many of the same features as *Creative Jazz Improvisation*, including

1. Easy-to-use divisions of each chapter into theoretical explanations, technical exercises, and repertoire
2. Special sections on *rhythm* and *how to practice and improvise*

Creative Beginnings differs, however, from the previous text in the following ways:

1. It eliminates transcribed solos, which, although valuable in the acquisition of jazz vocabulary, are often too difficult for less experienced musicians.
2. It includes theoretical discussions at the beginning of each chapter that assume little prior knowledge of the subject; musical terminology is italicized.
3. It provides beginning-to-advanced exercises, laid out in separate sections for each instrument.
4. It includes special chapters on "Whom to Listen To," "Music Theory," and "Jazz Theory."
5. Each chapter presents an original jazz composition, often based on a standard chord progression and form, arranged for any combination of instruments. This encourages the student to experience the act of improvisation as quickly as possible, while it teaches the basics of melody, harmony, rhythm, and form. These songs can be used during individual practice, improvisation class, and combo or big-band rehearsals.
6. There is a companion CD, which contains rhythm-section accompaniments to the warm-up progressions and compositions used in this text. The concept of

prerecorded rhythm-section accompaniments was pioneered by Jamey Aebersold in his play-along series, *A New Approach to Jazz Improvisation*. Several of the compositions in this text may also be performed along with selected volumes in Aebersold's series. The author gratefully acknowledges the inspiration of these play-along recordings and highly recommends their use in the teaching of improvisation.

Suggestions for the Jazz Band Director

It is hoped that directors will use this text as a warm-up to their ensemble rehearsal so that the students begin to develop improvisation skills in addition to learning written repertoire. One of the unique features of the art form of jazz is its reliance on improvisation, and therefore, the necessity of encouraging students to improvise cannot be overemphasized.

A typical jazz ensemble rehearsal could begin with a short explanation of a particular chord or scale, followed by a group performance of some of the warm-up exercises in all keys. Once the ensemble has achieved basic proficiency with the scale, individuals should try improvising on the chord progressions or scales being studied. The following rehearsal could be devoted to learning one of the songs at the end of each chapter. After playing the melody, the ensemble should practice some of the exercises that accompany the tune, then improvise on the song. You may find some of the compositions in this text appropriate for combo concerts and jazz festivals.

Chapters may be used in any order, at the discretion of the teacher or according to the needs of the student. Exercises are also listed in order of difficulty so that those most appropriate to the level of the student can be selected.

I sincerely hope that the reader will find this book to be a valuable aid in the study or teaching of jazz improvisation.

Scott D. Reeves

Improvisation is the courage to move from one note to the next. It's that simple. Once you conquer that basic fear, when you are able to make that leap from one note to the next without thinking or preparing for it, then you are improvising.

—vocalist Bobby McFerrin

CHAPTER

1

HOW TO PRACTICE
AND IMPROVISE

Learning to Hear

Improvisation means, simply, playing by ear. In learning to do this, we try to develop two things: (1) an awareness of pitches, scales, melodies, chords, and forms, and (2) the body's ability to produce those sounds on our chosen instrument.

Music is like any other language: It must be acquired through exposure and imitation. The only difference between the ability to recognize a major triad and the level of proficiency needed to recognize an altered dominant 7th chord is familiarity with the sound. Granted, there may be a genetic component that makes this process of assimilation quicker for some people, but most students, if not all, can expand their inner sense of hearing by repeated exposure to new sounds. You can develop these listening skills by

1. *Learning to control the workings of your mind.* Often, there is so much "inner noise" that we cannot concentrate or pay attention long enough to really hear the music.
2. *Spending some time each day listening to recordings by major jazz artists.* (Refer to the list in Chapter 2.) Listen with undivided attention instead of using the music as a background for your thoughts.
3. *Learning to play chords on the piano.* This develops your awareness of chords and harmonic progressions.
4. *Developing your ear* by practicing melodic/harmonic/rhythmic dictation, transcribing songs or improvised solos, and performing call-and-response exercises.

5. *Repeatedly practicing scales, chords, melodies, or transcriptions of improvised solos.* This will familiarize you with the jazz vocabulary. At some point, these sounds will become part of your own musical language, and you will become aware of their use when listening to other performers.

6. *Singing whatever you are working on,* even if you are not blessed with a great voice. Singing comes closest to immediately conveying what it is you are hearing. If you can't sing it, you probably won't be able to play it.

How to Practice

Once the ear begins to assimilate the jazz vocabulary, the next step is to play that vocabulary on an instrument. This is the hard part, because it requires practice and some discipline. Until there is "MIDI for the mind," and thoughts can be directly conveyed into sound, we have to train the body to respond to the ear. This is typically accomplished by playing certain scales, ideas, or melodies repeatedly until the appropriate motion becomes instinctive. At this point, your analytical mind might tell you that such repetitious practice will somehow dampen your creativity and spontaneity. That will not happen as long as you realize that the purpose of practicing is to remove the barriers to your creativity, not to learn a certain number of "hot licks" with which to amaze the public. Once your body knows what to do, your conscious mind can get out of the way and let your inner voice take over. If you do not practice the vocabulary to the point of being on "automatic pilot," you will flounder in your attempts to improvise: Either you will have nothing to play that remotely fits the underlying structure of the song, or you will play the most pedestrian "licks" that happen to comfortably come from your untrained fingers. Insufficient time spent practicing hampers creativity by not allowing the spirit to soar over familiar paths; you become confused or panicky, or you rely too much on your intellect to come up with a solution.

Guidelines for Practicing

1. *Practice at a slow enough tempo to stay physically relaxed and mentally concentrated on the sound.* Guard against any tension that might creep in and cause rhythmic problems or technical difficulties. Material learned in this manner can always be speeded up during successive repetitions.

2. *Once you have studied the theoretical concepts, rely on your ear and your instincts when practicing and improvising.* The intellectual part of your brain is too slow and predictable. It should aid your creativity and spontaneity, not get in the way. Don't get hung up in thinking about what you are practicing.

3. *Spend some portion of your practice session working on*

   a. *scales, chord arpeggios, or patterns*
   b. *transcriptions of improvised solos*
   c. *improvising on standard jazz literature*

Each of these skills develops your mastery of the jazz vocabulary in a slightly different way, and each is valuable. When practicing scales, arpeggios, or patterns, try to make the exercises as melodically and rhythmically interesting as possible; otherwise, practice may become dry and predictable. You can practice with a metronome clicking on beats 2 and 4 or with the CD that accompanies this book.

4. *Practice everything until your body has a "memory" of notes, so that you do not have to consciously think about them.*

How to Construct an Improvised Solo

Once your ear has been developed and your body programmed to respond accordingly, you can explore the construction of an improvised solo. Scales, arpeggios, and patterns are the raw materials from which a solo is built, but it is not always easy to make the shift from playing scales to creating an interesting musical statement. The following suggestions can aid in making that transition.

1. *Play along with recordings by master improvisors.* Much of the style, melodic and harmonic vocabulary, rhythmic interpretation, and the nuances of the language can be acquired in this manner.

2. *Develop a keen awareness of the form of the song.* You can do this by learning to feel the lengths of the phrases and by hearing the melody in your head while listening to or improvising on the song.

3. Many great jazz artists, such as Lester Young, Paul Desmond, Chet Baker, and Lee Konitz, emphasize the melody in their improvisations. Others, such as Coleman Hawkins and John Coltrane, tend to play more off the harmony. Some musicians, such as Louis Armstrong and Charlie Parker, seem to use both elements about equally. Experiment with these approaches by trying the following:

    a. *Melodic improvisation.* Improvise on the melody of the tune, adding embellishments and commentary, without losing the core of the song.

    b. *Guide-tone improvisation.* Guide tones are chord tones, typically the 3rds and the 7ths, that convey the quality of the chord, thus "guiding" you through the chord changes. For any given chord progression, you can construct guide-tone lines by starting on either the 3rd or the 7th of the first chord and moving to the 3rd or the 7th of the next chord, whichever is closer. The guide tone should be of the same duration as the chord. Extend this practice by creating an improvisation based on your embellishments of the guide tones.

    c. *Harmonic improvisation.* Outline the chord progression of the song with the arpeggios and scales that fit each chord, making sure each scale or arpeggio is of the same duration as the chord it colors. Then improvise on the song, freely playing off the chords.

4. The interpretation of a melody, particularly a "standard" or a ballad, can be considered a form of improvisation. *Listen to great song interpreters,* especially singers such as Sarah Vaughan, Carmen McRae, and Betty Carter, to see how they play with the rhythm and phrasing of a melody.

5. *Motivic improvisation.* Make up one short melodic idea or motive, and use it as the basis for at least eight measures of improvisation. Expand and develop the motive to create new material. Sometimes you can transpose the idea up or down (called sequencing) to fit a new chord. Some great improvisors, such as Thelonious Monk, Sonny Rollins, and J. J. Johnson, are highly motivic in their playing, whereas others, such as Bud Powell and Charlie Parker, seem to spin out a continuous melody.

6. *Rhythmic improvisation.* Experiment with a variety of articulations and accents, as well as the contrast between long and short notes. It might be helpful to think of the rhythms first and add the pitches as an afterthought. Try playing a solo using just one or two notes, letting rhythms provide the interest.

7. *Be aware of phrasing and space.* Always hear your improvised lines as a melody having a definite beginning and ending, not just as a series of notes. Avoid playing too many notes or "running on." Think of your solo as a dialogue with the other musicians, and leave spaces for their responses to your ideas. One of the outstanding aspects of Miles Davis's group of the mid-1960s was this use of space and group dialogue.

How to Improvise Creatively

If you develop your ear, diligently practice the raw materials of the jazz vocabulary, and learn to put together a coherent improvised solo, you will have achieved a level of competence as an improvisor. It is possible, however, to go beyond craftsmanship to a level of artistry that draws from a deeper well of creativity. This mode of thought is seldom taught in schools, because it is not easy to analyze or describe. Concepts such as the "superconscious" and "right brain/left brain" thinking, and certain mental states described by various religious and cultures, all point to the same goal. Essentially, everything you have learned or practiced that has led you to this point must be left behind. Once you have learned a song, improvise on the tune without looking at or thinking about the chords or the notes. *Trust your body programming to take care of the notes, and let your feelings and imagination take over.* Above all, LISTEN, LISTEN, LISTEN.

CHAPTER

2

WHOM TO LISTEN TO

The importance of listening to great jazz artists cannot be overemphasized. Your melodic, harmonic, and rhythmic abilities can be developed by listening to and playing along with the recordings of the masters. As you build your collection of recordings, you will also develop an awareness and an appreciation of the diversity of styles and the historical evolution of this music.

Although there are hundreds of great players and stylists, the list in this chapter is limited to those individuals (in this author's opinion) whose influence has been the most pervasive in each style for the greatest period of time. Thus, many of the younger artists now emerging are omitted, but they are well worth listening to. Women, while traditionally underrepresented as instrumentalists, are now beginning to exert greater influence on the development of contemporary jazz. Make sure to listen to a wide range of instrumentalists and singers, regardless of what instrument you happen to play.

Visit your school or local library and see which jazz recordings are available. Many libraries have the *Smithsonian Collection of Classic Jazz*, which provides a good overview of the historical range of styles. If you go to your local record store to purchase CDs or cassettes, be aware that some of the musicians marketed as jazz artists are actually in the pop idiom. Also notice that although many artists cultivate a style and stay with it throughout their lifetime, some musicians, such as Duke Ellington, Miles Davis, and John Coltrane, have gradually or radically changed their approach. For these people, it will be necessary to listen to recordings from different periods of their career to develop an appreciation of their work. For convenience, this list is divided by instruments or genres and is generally chronological.

Big Bands

1. *Duke Ellington.* A great composer–pianist, whose bands from the late 1920s to the early 1970s reflected his genius. He was one of the few jazz composers to write longer, more involved works, such as suites, movie soundtracks, and sacred music.

2. *Count Basie.* From its Kansas City beginnings in the 1930s to the present edition, the Basie band has been synonymous with swing. Simplicity, a strong blues feeling, and great soloists are characteristic of the Basie tradition.

3. *Benny Goodman.* A great clarinetist, whose big bands and small groups from the '30s and '40s demonstrate how he balanced polished precision with spontaneity and swing.

4. *Woody Herman.* Another clarinetist, best known for his bebop-oriented bands of the '40s and '50s and his more contemporary "herds" of the '60s and '70s. One of Herman's talents was his knack for selecting the best young players and allowing them to find their own voice.

5. *Stan Kenton.* A California-based pianist–bandleader who favored a heavy brass sound and experimented with modern harmonies and techniques borrowed from contemporary classical music. His greatest period of influence was from the 1940s to the 1970s.

6. *Thad Jones and Mel Lewis.* Cornetist Thad Jones and drummer Mel Lewis co-led a very contemporary, swinging band that featured many of New York's finest jazz musicians. Beginning in the 1960s, this group played every Monday at the Village Vanguard in Manhattan and has continued as the "Vanguard Orchestra" since the deaths of Thad and Mel. Thad Jones is considered one of the greatest big-band composers since Duke Ellington.

7. *Gil Evans.* An underrecorded arranger who introduced new instrumental colors into big-band writing. Some of his greatest works include his collaborations with Miles Davis in the late '50s and early '60s.

Clarinet/Bass Clarinet

1. *Benny Goodman.* (See under Big Bands.)
2. *Buddy DeFranco.* Brought the clarinet into the modern bebop style.
3. *Eric Dolphy.* A bass clarinetist–alto saxophonist–flautist who stretched the boundaries of jazz in the 1960s.
4. *Eddie Daniels.* A contemporary virtuoso on the clarinet.

Alto Saxophone

1. *Johnny Hodges.* Duke Ellington's lead alto player for many years. His beautiful tone and bent notes set the standard for swing-era alto players.

2. *Benny Carter.* A contemporary of Hodges; also a prolific composer and big bandleader.

3. *Charlie Parker.* The father of bebop and the greatest improvisor of his time, whose work in the '40s and early '50s influenced almost all instrumentalists who followed.

4. *Cannonball Adderley.* After his initial work with Miles Davis, Cannonball went on to lead a combo that successfully combined Parker's innovations with the soulful, funky hard-bop sound of the '60s and '70s.

5. *Phil Woods.* Also extended the Parker sound into more contemporary styles.

6. *Lee Konitz and Paul Desmond.* Both of these artists favored a light sound and a melodic approach to improvisation.

Tenor and Soprano Saxophone

1. *Coleman Hawkins.* Called the father of the tenor sax. His full sound and arpeggiated approach to improvisation dominated the 1930s.
2. *Lester Young.* Young's light tone and melodic approach presented an alternative to the Hawkins sound. His work with the Basie band of the '30s was a major influence on the cool and West Coast musicians of the '50s and '60s.
3. *Sonny Rollins.* The first major tenor saxophonist to embrace Parker's innovations. His playing from the 1950s to the present demonstrates great spontaneity and rhythmic vitality.
4. *Stan Getz.* Getz's warm sound and lyrical style helped popularize the cool and Brazilian-influenced styles of the '50s and '60s.
5. *John Coltrane.* An intense, searching musician who created the modal/pentatonic vocabulary of the '60s and was also active in free jazz before his death in 1967. Coltrane is a major influence on many of the younger tenor and soprano saxophonists of the '70s, '80s, and '90s.
6. *Wayne Shorter.* Shorter's work with Art Blakey, Miles Davis, and Weather Report, as well as his many wonderful compositions, established him as one of the preeminent soprano and tenor saxophonists of the past three decades.
7. *Michael Brecker and David Liebman.* Contemporary players who successfully blend the Coltrane vocabulary with elements from fusion jazz.
8. *Joe Lovano.* A modern extension of the Rollins/Coltrane lineage.

Baritone Saxophone

1. *Harry Carney.* Ellington's mainstay for many decades.
2. *Gerry Mulligan.* Embraced Lester Young's lighter approach and was instrumental in the development of cool jazz in the '50s and '60s.
3. *Pepper Adams and Nick Brignola.* Personify the New York hard-bop sound of the '50s, '60s, and '70s.

Trumpet/Cornet/Flugelhorn

1. *Louis Armstrong.* Acknowledged as the first great improvisor in jazz. His playing in the '20s and '30s set the standard for all other jazz musicians.
2. *Roy Eldridge.* Eldridge's work during the swing era of the 1930s extended the Armstrong concept and paved the way for bebop artists such as Dizzy Gillespie.
3. *Dizzy Gillespie.* Along with Parker, one of the inventors of the 1940s style known as bebop. Besides being a great trumpet player, he popularized modern jazz through his entertaining and colorful personality and introduced Latin rhythms into jazz.
4. *Clifford Brown.* Although Brown's career was cut tragically short with his death at age 26, his exceptional fluency on the instrument extended the bebop vocabulary during the early 1950s.
5. *Clark Terry.* Terry's wit, warm sound, and buoyant musical personality made the flugelhorn a popular solo instrument.
6. *Miles Davis.* A great musical visionary as well as a trumpet player, Miles led the way in five different styles of jazz: bebop, cool, hard bop, free jazz, and fusion.

His two quintets of the '50s and '60s are widely acknowledged to be among the most influential groups in modern jazz.

7. *Freddie Hubbard and Lee Morgan.* Trumpet players who extended the Clifford Brown legacy into the '60s and '70s.

8. *Woody Shaw.* An underappreciated trumpet player who not only mastered the bebop vocabulary but also applied contemporary concepts such as wide intervals and pentatonic scales to the trumpet.

9. *Wynton Marsalis.* Marsalis's talent as a jazz prodigy was responsible for attracting greater media attention to jazz. Recently, he has encouraged the development of a "neo-classical" movement in jazz, in which younger artists are investigating styles from the '20s and '30s.

Trombone

1. *Jack Teagarden.* The "Louis Armstrong of trombone," whose wit and fluency on the instrument established the trombone as a major solo voice.

2. *Benny Green.* A swing player from the 1930s who paved the way for the bebop style of J. J. Johnson.

3. *J. J. Johnson.* The person chiefly responsible for figuring out how to apply the language of bebop to the trombone.

4. *Curtis Fuller and Slide Hampton.* Extended J. J.'s innovations.

5. *Albert Mangelsdorff.* A German trombonist rooted in the J. J. tradition but known for experimenting with contemporary techniques such as *multiphonics* (singing and playing simultaneously to produce chords).

6. *Carl Fontana and Frank Rosolino.* West Coast virtuosos who extended the technical possibilities of the trombone.

Violin

1. *Stephane Grappelli.* An elegant stylist rooted in the swing tradition of the 1930s.

2. *Jean-Luc Ponty.* A French violinist active in the contemporary fusion style.

Guitar

1. *Django Reinhardt.* A Belgian guitarist known for his work with Stephane Grappelli in the 1930s.

2. *Charlie Christian.* As a member of the Benny Goodman small group of the late '30s and early '40s, Christian paved the way for the hard-bop guitarists who followed.

3. *Wes Montgomery.* This master of '50s hard bop set the standard for modern jazz guitar. His octave melodies became his trademark sound.

4. *Joe Pass.* A bebop guitarist with a prodigious technique and a warm sound.

5. *John McLaughlin.* An English guitarist who played fusion with Miles Davis in the '70s and continues to explore new approaches to jazz, embracing influences from Indian and other Third World musics.

6. *Pat Metheny and John Scofield.* These two contemporary masters draw on bebop roots but combine the best of fusion, free jazz, and other modern styles into their own personal sound.

Piano

1. *Jelly Roll Morton.* An early jazz pianist who was considered the first important jazz composer.

2. *Art Tatum.* A true virtuoso. The work of this blind pianist during the 1930s influenced generations of jazz pianists and drew the admiration of classical pianists as well.

3. *Bud Powell.* Through his mastery of the instrument, Powell was able to apply Charlie Parker's innovations to the piano during the '40s and '50s.

4. *Thelonious Monk.* A contemporary of Powell's but a very different type of pianist. Instead of displaying virtuoso technique, Monk drew on his great skill as a composer and a wonderfully unpredictable approach to improvisation.

5. *Horace Silver.* Best known as a hard-bop composer and small-group leader, he introduced soulful and funky elements into modern jazz.

6. *Bill Evans.* A sensitive pianist with a singing tone. In the '60s and '70s, Evans revolutionized the concept of the piano trio, giving each member of the group an equal voice.

7. *McCoy Tyner.* Coltrane's pianist from 1960 to 1965, Tyner integrated pentatonic scales and voicings in 4ths with a powerful approach to the instrument.

8. *Keith Jarrett.* A contemporary player who defies categorization, drawing on hard bop, fusion, free jazz, European classical, gospel, and other idioms to create an extremely personal, emotionally profound style.

9. *Herbie Hancock and Chick Corea.* These pianists (as well as Silver, Evans, and Jarrett) were important members of Miles Davis's groups. Both continue to alternate between contemporary acoustic jazz and electronic fusion styles.

Vibraphone

1. *Lionel Hampton.* Through his recordings with Benny Goodman's ground-breaking swing combo and his own big band, Hampton established the vibes as a popular jazz instrument.

2. *Milt Jackson.* Jackson's elegant, bluesy performances with the Modern Jazz Quartet serve as the standard for bebop vibraphonists.

3. *Gary Burton.* A contemporary player whose pioneering work with four-mallet techniques opened up new ways of playing the instrument.

4. *Bobby Hutcherson.* Like his colleagues Woody Shaw and McCoy Tyner, Hutcherson participated in the post-Coltrane style.

Bass

1. *Milt Hinton.* An important bassist during the 1930s, Hinton continues to be active and modern-sounding in the '90s.

2. *Jimmy Blanton.* Ellington's bassist during the late '30s and early '40s. He paved the way for the bebop stylists that followed.

3. *Oscar Pettiford.* Established the bass as a bebop instrument during the 1940s.

4. *Charles Mingus.* An energetic bandleader–composer, as well as an important bassist from the 1940s to the 1970s.

5. *Paul Chambers.* A member of the Miles Davis quintet of the mid-to-late '50s, Chambers was a virtuoso soloist known for his use of the bow.

6. *Scott LaFaro.* A member of the influential Bill Evans trio of the early 1960s. Until his premature death, LaFaro was known for his conversational approach to bass lines and his hornlike solos. He is a major influence on contemporary players such as Eddie Gomez and Gary Peacock.

7. *Jaco Pastorius.* Pastorius made the fretless electric bass a viable jazz instrument with his stunning technique and imagination.

Drums

1. *Baby Dodds.* Armstrong's drummer during the 1920s. He was one of the first significant performers on his instrument.
2. *Gene Krupa.* Krupa's strong drive was an important element in the Benny Goodman big band and small groups of the '30s and '40s, and a major influence on later drummers, such as Buddy Rich.
3. *Jo Jones.* The man who swung the swingingest band of its day—the Basie band of the 1930s.
4. *Max Roach and Kenny Clarke.* The first two drummers to apply bebop innovations to their instrument. Roach continues to be active in the '90s, playing a freer style of jazz.
5. *Art Blakey.* A powerful drummer known for leading the Jazz Messengers and discovering many major talents from the '50s through the '80s.
6. *Elvin Jones.* Coltrane's drummer from 1960 to 1965. His powerful, polyrhythmic playing continues to be influential.
7. *Tony Williams and Jack DeJohnette.* Contemporary drummers who were important components in Miles Davis's bands. Both have combined technical independence with imaginative concepts to create new approaches to the drums.

Vocalists

1. *Louis Armstrong.* The first great "scat" singer. His wit, graciousness, and infectious swing touched listeners around the world.
2. *Billie Holiday.* Billie's great depth of emotion and laid-back phrasing makes her recordings from the '30s and '40s sound fresh even today.
3. *Ella Fitzgerald.* Beginning with her early work with Chick Webb's band in the 1930s, and continuing for several decades, Ella's style has been synonymous with swing and hornlike phrasing.
4. *Sarah Vaughan.* Sarah possessed a fantastic "instrument," and her sound and control were universally admired.
5. *Betty Carter.* The epitome of the bebop singer, Carter improvises with melody and phrasing to an unprecedented degree. From the 1960s to the present, she has discovered and employed many promising young musicians.
6. *Joe Williams.* A singer with Count Basie's band for many years, Williams is renowned for his swinging, bluesy style.
7. *Bobby McFerrin.* A contemporary singer of unbridled imagination. Jazz is too small a category to contain all his ideas.

CHAPTER

3

JAZZ RHYTHMS

Rhythm is the most important element of jazz. The *swing feeling* or *groove* is what gives jazz its unique personality and mood. Without a strong rhythmic underpinning, melodies, chords, and scales have little meaning.

Jazz rhythms are derived primarily from African music. In America, jazz rhythms also drew on marching-band cadences, ragtime, gospel music, and blues. Jazz rhythms are characterized by

1. *Syncopation* (tying the notes on the offbeats to notes on the downbeat). Jazz melodies also typically start and end on offbeats.

   In the preceding example, the melody begins and ends on the offbeat (the & of 1 and the & of 4, respectively). The offbeats are also accented.

2. *Polyrhythms* (more than one rhythm or meter occurring simultaneously). In the following example, Louis Armstrong implied a 3/8 meter by playing a note every 1½ beats while the rhythm section played in 4/4.[1]

---

[1]From Louis Armstrong's improvised solo on "Hotter Than That," composed by Lil Hardin Armstrong. In Scott D. Reeves, *Creative Jazz Improvisation*, 2nd ed. (Englewood Cliffs, N.J.: Prentice Hall, 1995), pp. 21–28.

3. *Accents on beats 2 and 4.* Music that has evolved from African-American culture, such as blues, gospel, funk, soul, rap, and jazz, contains a strong accent on beats 2 and 4 in a 4/4 meter. When listening to these styles of music, notice the emphasis placed on these beats by the snare drum, the hi-hat cymbal, and hand clapping. In styles derived from European music, beats 2 and 4 are usually thought of as weak beats and are not stressed.

4. *Swing*—perhaps jazz's most identifiable trait. Jazz "swings" when the eighth notes are played in an uneven, long-short manner. Depending on the tempo, this lopsided division of the eighth note can range from nearly even to a 2-to-1 ratio (like triplets with the first two notes tied).

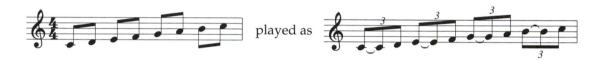

In general, the offbeats are also accented, as if you were saying "doo-BAH" or "ooo-DAH."

Most, but not all, styles of jazz swing. In Latin and fusion jazz styles, the eighth notes are typically played evenly. You can develop these concepts by listening to and playing along with recordings by great jazz artists.

5. *Articulations and tone decorations.* The way the notes are articulated or personalized conveys the rhythmic feeling as well as the emotions of the performer. In the following example, the notes on the beat are played short, and the two consecutive eighth notes ending on the offbeat are played "long-short"(∧ indicates a short accent).

Continuous eighth notes are typically played long (legato), until the last note, which is short.

These articulations may not be marked in the music, but they should be felt and interpreted as such by the performer.

Jazz musicians also employ other types of articulations, sometimes referred to as *tone decorations*, such as the *fall-off* (dropping down from the note):

the *doit* (rising upward from the note):

the *scoop* or *glissando* (bending up to the pitch):

ghosted notes (notes that do not completely sound, or "speak"—indicated by an **X**):

bent or *"blue" notes* (notes between normal scale tones), and *half-valve notes* (played with the valves on the trumpet pressed halfway down).

Feel free to use these and other ways of personalizing your sound when you improvise.

RHYTHM WARM-UPS

1. *Latin Rhythms*

    a. Play this exercise over the following chord progression, using either a metronome, a live rhythm section, or the "Rhythm Warm-Ups: Latin Rhythms" play-along track on the companion CD.

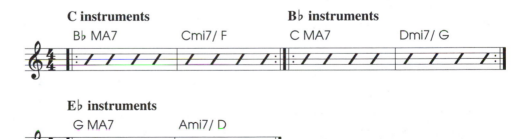

b. Clap and sing the following rhythms and articulations.

Latin

c. Improvise a solo using the preceding rhythms and the notes in the following *major pentatonic scale*. Start with one pitch, and gradually add the remaining notes as you become comfortable with the rhythm.

Treble clef C instruments   **B♭ instruments**

E♭ instruments   **Bass clef instruments**

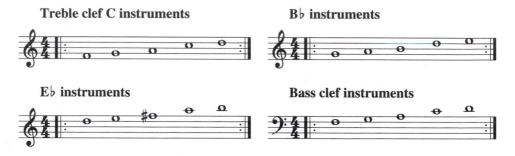

2. *Swing Rhythms*

a. Play this exercise over the following chord progression, using either a metronome, a live rhythm section, or the "Rhythm Warm-Ups: Swing Rhythms" play-along track on the companion CD. (On the CD, the chord progression is played seven times.)

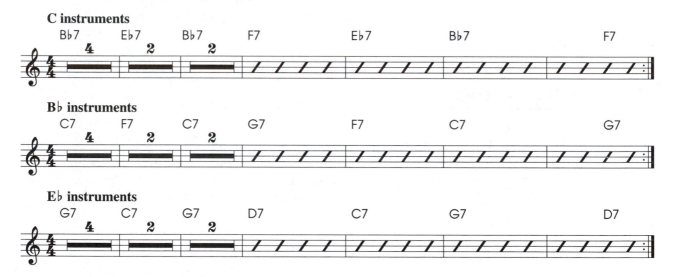

b. Clap and sing the following rhythms and articulations.

Swing *(Notes in parentheses are ghosted or played very softly.)*

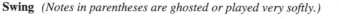

c. Improvise a solo using the preceding rhythms and the notes in the following *blues scale.* Start with one pitch, and gradually add the remaining notes as you become comfortable with the rhythm.

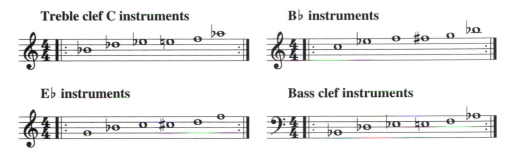

All Instruments—Improvisation Exercises

1. Improvise over the preceding chord progressions, using the scales given. Use strong rhythmic ideas, and develop them into coherent, singable phrases. Be sure to listen to the rhythm section.
2. Make up your own exercises based on strong rhythmic motives.

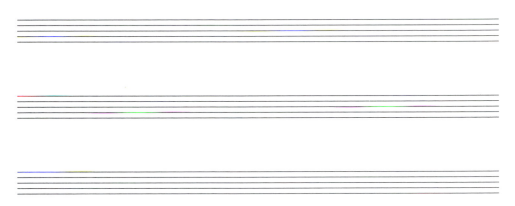

Sometimes I'm able to step outside myself and hear what I'm playing. The ideas just flow. The horn and I become one.

—tenor saxophonist Sonny Rollins

4

MAJOR SCALES AND MAJOR 7TH CHORDS

The ascending *major scale* consists of the following pattern of whole steps and half steps: whole, whole, half, whole, whole, whole, half.

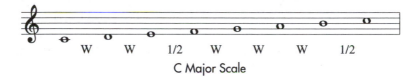

C Major Scale

The sound of the major scale is familiar to most musicians, since it probably is the first scale they learned. It is usually associated with happy, upbeat songs, such as "Frère Jacques," "Do-Re-Mi" (from *The Sound of Music*), "America the Beautiful," and "Over the Rainbow" (from *The Wizard of Oz*).

You can use the notes of the major scale when improvising over *major 7th chords*. Major 7th chords are made up of the first, third, fifth, and seventh notes in the major scale. These notes are referred to as the *root*, the *major 3rd*, the *perfect 5th*, and the *major 7th* of the chord.[1]

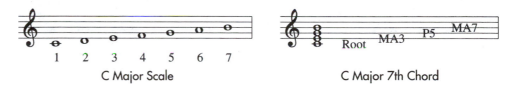

C Major Scale   C Major 7th Chord

[1]Refer to Chapter 14 for further information on intervals.

It is also possible to extend the major 7th chord by adding the *major 9th* and the *major 13th* (the second and the sixth notes of the scale an octave higher, respectively). The *augmented 11th* (the fourth note of the major scale raised a half step, up an octave) may also be added to the major 7th chord. This note is a member of the *lydian scale,* which is also used when improvising over major 7th chords, particularly when either the ♯11th or the ♯4th (or its enharmonic equivalent, the ♭5th) is added to the chord.

Major 7th chords have a pretty, lush, or romantic quality. Adding the 9th, the ♯11, and the 13th to the chord enriches the warm quality of the major 7th chord and adds a touch of exoticism to the sound. Listen to jazz standards such as "Misty," "I'm Getting Sentimental Over You," "Early Autumn," and "I Can't Get Started,"[2] which spell out the sound of the chord in their opening phrases. Also try singing major scales and major 7th chord arpeggios and playing major 7th chords on the piano.

Major Scale Warm-Ups

Play the following exercises over the chord progression, using either a metronome, a live rhythm section, or the "Major Scale Warm-Ups" play-along track on the companion CD. Play the written example over the first chord; then use your ear to play the exercise in the different keys indicated by the chord symbols. You will find it helpful to look at the chord progression instead of the exercises when playing in the remaining eleven keys. Pick a tempo at which you can effortlessly play each exercise, gradually moving on to more difficult exercises after you have mastered the easier ones.

Treble Clef C Instruments—Chord Progression

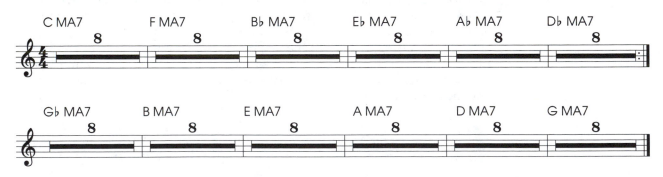

[2]The music to these songs may be found in the following volumes of *A New Approach to Jazz Improvisation:* "Misty" (Vol. 41), "I'm Getting Sentimental Over You" (Vol. 42), "Early Autumn" (Vol. 40), "I Can't Get Started" (Vol. 25).

Treble Clef C Instruments—Beginning Exercises

1. The first five notes of the major scale:

2. The complete scale, ascending:

Treble Clef C Instruments—Intermediate Exercises

3. The complete scale, descending:

4. A melodic fragment similar to "St. Thomas" by Sonny Rollins.[3]

5. The basic major 7th arpeggio:

[3]Sonny Rollins, "St. Thomas," copyright 1963 by Prestige Music.

Treble Clef C Instruments—Advanced Exercises

6. An arpeggio similar to the beginning of "I'm Getting Sentimental Over You."[4]

7. The scale in thirds:

B♭ Instruments—Chord Progression

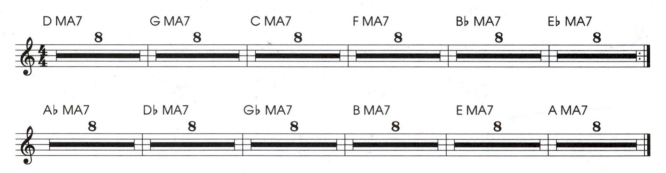

B♭ Instruments—Beginning Exercises

1. The first five notes of the major scale:

2. The complete scale, ascending:

[4]George Bassman, "I'm Getting Sentimental Over You," copyright 1932 by Mills Music.

B♭ Instruments—Intermediate Exercises

3. The complete scale, descending:

4. A melodic fragment similar to "St. Thomas" by Sonny Rollins.

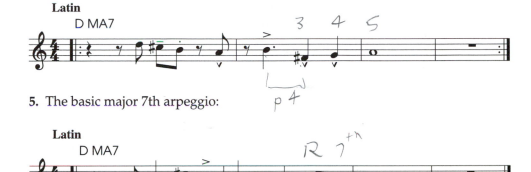

5. The basic major 7th arpeggio:

B♭ Instruments—Advanced Exercises

6. An arpeggio similar to the beginning of "I'm Getting Sentimental Over You."

7. The scale in thirds:

E♭ Instruments—Chord Progression

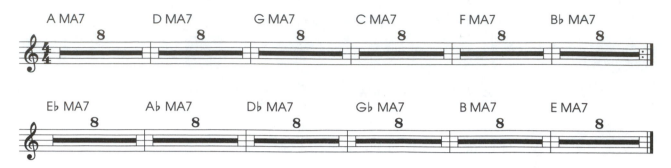

E♭ Instruments—Beginning Exercises

1. The first five notes of the major scale:

2. The complete scale, ascending:

E♭ Instruments—Intermediate Exercises

3. The complete scale, descending:

4. A melodic fragment similar to "St. Thomas" by Sonny Rollins.

5. The basic major 7th arpeggio:

E♭ Instruments—Advanced Exercises

6. An arpeggio similar to the beginning of "I'm Getting Sentimental Over You."

7. The scale in thirds:

Bass Clef Instruments—Chord Progression

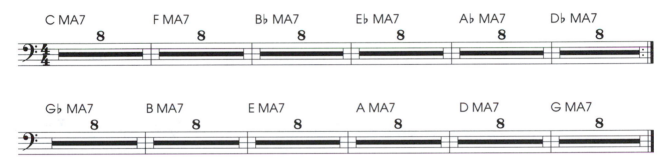

Bass Clef Instruments—Beginning Exercises

1. The first five notes of the major scale:

2. The complete scale, ascending:

Bass Clef Instruments—Intermediate Exercises

3. The complete scale, descending:

4. A melodic fragment similar to "St. Thomas" by Sonny Rollins.

5. The basic major 7th arpeggio:

Bass Clef Instruments—Advanced Exercises

6. An arpeggio similar to the beginning of "I'm Getting Sentimental Over You."

7. The scale in thirds:

All Instruments—Improvisation Exercises

1. Improvise on major 7th chords in all keys, using a live rhythm section or the "Major Scale Warm-ups" play-along track on the companion CD.
2. Make up your own exercises and melodic ideas based on major scales and major 7th chords.

Jmprovising on Major 7th Chords

"Another Spring" is a composition based on major 7th chords. Practice and improvise on the song, using either a metronome, a live rhythm section, or the "Another Spring" play-along track on the companion CD. (On the CD, the chord progression is played five times.)

After playing the melody, practice the chord progression by outlining the chords with the exercises that follow the song. After singing each example, *sequence* it over the different chords in the progression, making sure each sequence is eight measures long.[5]

---

[5]A sequence is a melodic idea whose basic shape repeats but whose notes may be altered to fit the new chord.

Another Spring

Treble Clef C Instruments

Swing

Scott Reeves

Treble Clef Instruments—Exercises for "Another Spring."

Transpose each exercise to fit the other chords of the song.

1. A paraphrase of warm-up 1:

2. The complete scale, ascending:

3. The complete scale, descending:

4. A paraphrase of the "St. Thomas" fragment:

5. The basic major 7th arpeggio:

6. A paraphrase of the "Sentimental" arpeggio:

7. The scale in thirds:

Another Spring

B♭ Instruments

Swing

Scott Reeves

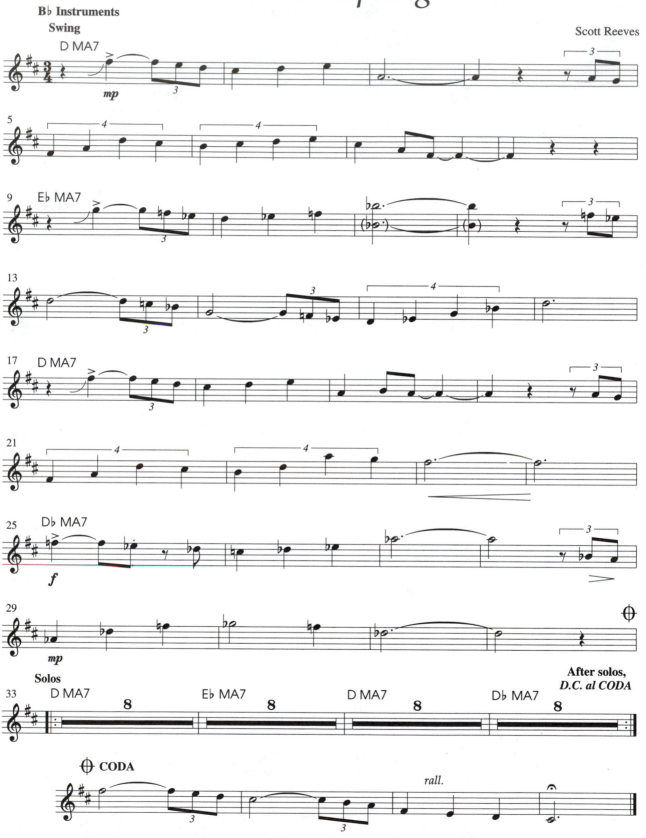

B♭ Instruments—Exercises for "Another Spring."

Transpose each exercise to fit the other chords of the song.

1. A paraphrase of warm-up 1:

D MA7

2. The complete scale, ascending:

D MA7

3. The complete scale, descending:

D MA7

4. A paraphrase of the "St. Thomas" fragment:

D MA7

5. The basic major 7th arpeggio:

D MA7

6. A paraphrase of the "Sentimental" arpeggio:

D MA7

7. The scale in thirds:

D MA7

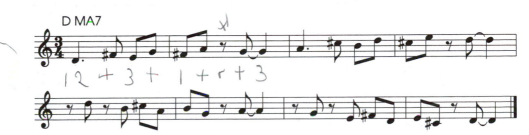

Another Spring

E♭ Instruments
Swing

Scott Reeves

E♭ Instruments—Exercises for "Another Spring."

Transpose each exercise to fit the other chords of the song.

1. A paraphrase of warm-up 1:

2. The complete scale, ascending:

3. The complete scale, descending:

4. A paraphrase of the "St. Thomas" fragment:

5. The basic major 7th arpeggio:

6. A paraphrase of the "Sentimental" arpeggio:

7. The scale in thirds:

Another Spring

Bass Clef Instruments
Swing

Scott Reeves

Bass Clef Instruments—Exercises for "Another Spring."

Transpose each exercise to fit the other chords of the song.

1. A paraphrase of warm-up 1:

C MA7

2. The complete scale, ascending:

C MA7

3. The complete scale, descending:

C MA7

4. A paraphrase of the "St. Thomas" fragment:

C MA7

5. The basic major 7th arpeggio:

C MA7

6. A paraphrase of the "Sentimental" arpeggio:

C MA7

7. The scale in thirds:

C MA7

Another Spring

Another Spring

Scott Reeves

CHAPTER

5

MIXOLYDIAN AND BEBOP 7TH SCALES AND DOMINANT 7TH CHORDS

The *mixolydian scale* can be thought of as a major scale with a lowered 7th.

C Mixolydian Scale   C Major Scale

The mixolydian scale also contains the same notes as the major scale a perfect 5th below.

C Mixolydian Scale   F Major Scale

The *bebop 7th scale* is made up of the same notes as the mixolydian scale but adds the major 7th, creating a scale with nine notes to the octave.

C Bebop 7th Scale

This scale is called the bebop 7th scale because it came into widespread use during the bebop era of the 1940s. Both the mixolydian and the bebop 7th scales have a "jazzy" quality and are used when improvising over *dominant 7th chords*. Dominant 7th chords are made up of the first, third, fifth, and seventh notes of the mixolydian scale. These notes are called the *root*, the *major 3rd*, the *perfect 5th*, and the *minor 7th* of the chord.[1] Notice that the dominant 7th chord is the same as a major 7th chord with the 7th lowered one half step.

C Dominant 7th Chord   C Major 7th Chord

The dominant 7th chord is often extended by adding the second and the sixth notes of the mixolydian scale an octave higher (called the *major 9th* and the *major 13th* of the chord, respectively). The fourth note of the scale may also be added to the dominant 7th chord, but the note must either be raised a half step (called the *augmented 11th* of the chord) or be used in place of the 3rd of the chord (known as a *dominant 7th sus. 4 chord*). Notice that the symbol for a dominant 7th chord does not use the word "dominant."

C9   C13   C#11   C7sus.4

Dominant 7th chords have strong, biting, bluesy qualities, particularly when *chord extensions* are added. Many jazz songs in the blues form, such as Miles Davis's "Freddie Freeloader," Herbie Hancock's "Watermelon Man," and Charlie Parker's "Now's the Time," are composed largely of dominant 7th chords.[2] Before practicing the following exercises, try singing mixolydian and bebop 7th scales, as well as dominant 7th chord arpeggios. Also try playing dominant 7th chords in different keys on the piano.

---

[1] Refer to Chapter 14 for further information on intervals.

[2] The music to these songs may be found in the following volumes of *A New Approach to Jazz Improvisation*: "Freddie Freeloader" (Vol. 50), "Watermelon Man" (Vols. 54 and 11), and "Now's the Time" (Vol. 6).

MIXOLYDIAN AND BEBOP 7TH SCALE WARM-UPS

Play the following exercises over the chord progression, using either a metronome, a live rhythm section, or the "Mixolydian and Bebop 7th Scale Warm-Ups" play-along track on the companion CD. Play the written example over the first chord; then use your ear to play the exercise in the different keys indicated by the chord symbols. You will find it helpful to look at the chord progression instead of the exercises when playing in the remaining eleven keys. Pick a tempo at which you can effortlessly play each exercise, gradually moving on to more difficult exercises after you have mastered the easier ones.

Treble Clef C Instruments—Chord Progression

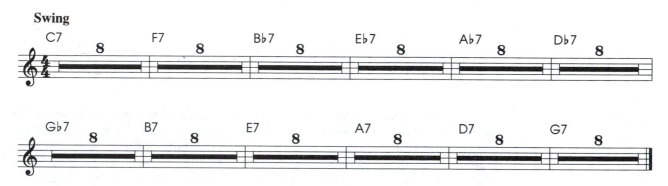

Treble Clef C Instruments—Beginning Exercises

1. The bebop 7th scale, from the root down to the 7th:

2. The bebop 7th scale, from the root down to the 5th:

3. The bebop 7th scale, descending:

Treble Clef C Instruments—Intermediate Exercises

4. The bebop 7th scale, ascending:

5. The bebop 7th scale, descending from the 3rd to the 7th:

Treble Clef C Instruments—Advanced Exercises

6. The dominant 9th arpeggio, ascending from the 3rd:

7. The bebop 7th scale with a chromatic passing tone, descending from the 3rd:

8. The mixolydian and bebop 7th scales, descending from the 9th:

B♭ Instruments—Chord Progression

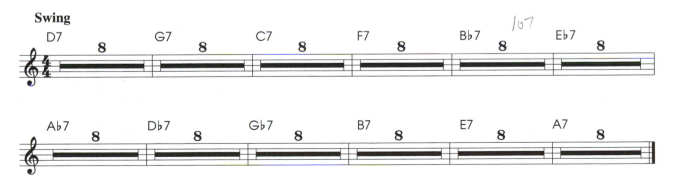

B♭ Instruments—Beginning Exercises

1. The bebop 7th scale, from the root down to the 7th:

2. The bebop 7th scale, from the root down to the 5th:

3. The bebop 7th scale, descending:

B♭ Instruments—Intermediate Exercises

4. The bebop 7th scale, ascending:

5. The bebop 7th scale, descending from the 3rd to the 7th:

B♭ Instruments—Advanced Exercises

6. The dominant 9th arpeggio, ascending from the 3rd:

7. The bebop 7th scale with a chromatic passing tone, descending from the 3rd:

8. The mixolydian and bebop 7th scales, descending from the 9th:

E♭ Instruments—Chord Progression

Swing

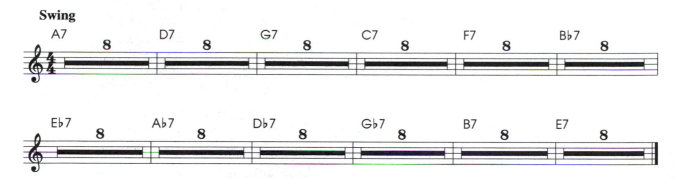

E♭ Instruments—Beginning Exercises

1. The bebop 7th scale, from the root down to the 7th:

2. The bebop 7th scale, from the root down to the 5th:

3. The bebop 7th scale, descending:

E♭ Instruments—Intermediate Exercises

4. The bebop 7th scale, ascending:

5. The bebop 7th scale, descending from the 3rd to the 7th:

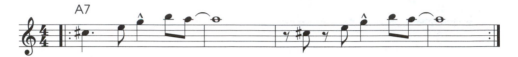

E♭ Instruments—Advanced Exercises

6. The dominant 9th arpeggio, ascending from the 3rd:

7. The bebop 7th scale with a chromatic passing tone, descending from the 3rd:

8. The mixolydian and bebop 7th scales, descending from the 9th:

Bass Clef Instruments—Chord Progression

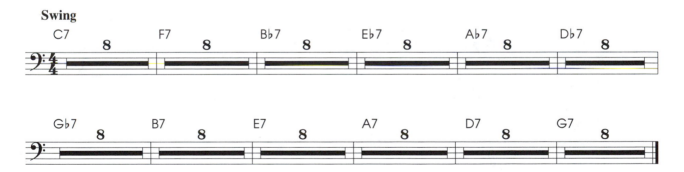

Bass Clef Instruments—Beginning Exercises

1. The bebop 7th scale, from the root down to the 7th:

2. The bebop 7th scale, from the root down to the 5th:

3. The bebop 7th scale, descending:

Bass Clef Instruments—Intermediate Exercises

4. The bebop 7th scale, ascending:

5. The bebop 7th scale, descending from the 3rd to the 7th:

Bass Clef Instruments—Advanced Exercises

6. The dominant 9th arpeggio, ascending from the 3rd:

7. The bebop 7th scale with a chromatic passing tone, descending from the 3rd:

8. The mixolydian and bebop 7th scales, descending from the 9th:

All Instruments—Improvisation Exercises

1. Improvise on dominant 7th chords in all keys, using a live rhythm section or the "Mixolydian and Bebop 7th Scale Warm-Ups" track on the companion CD.

2. Make up your own exercises and melodic ideas based on mixolydian and bebop 7th scales or dominant 7th chords.

Improvising on Dominant 7th Chords

"Sister Cynda" is a composition based on dominant 7th chords. Practice and improvise on the song, using either a metronome, a live rhythm section, or the "Sister Cynda" play-along track on the companion CD. (On the CD, the chord progression is played six times.)

"Sister Cynda" is based on the chord progression to a Horace Silver song, "Sister Sadie."[3] The structure of the song is referred to as an *AABA form,* in which each letter represents an 8-bar phrase.[4] The melody of the A section is based on a triplet idea that repeats with variations, and the B section consists of a syncopated rhythmic figure. The A section contains a single dominant 7th chord lasting eight measures, whereas the chords in the B section change every bar or every two bars. A song in which the chords last at least four measures is called a *modal* tune. "Sister Cynda" combines a modal A section with a B section based on faster chord changes.

After playing the melody, practice the chord progression by outlining the chords with the exercises that follow the song. Play the entire exercise over the chords lasting four bars, play the first half of each exercise over the chords lasting two bars, and play the first measure of the exercise over the chords lasting one bar, as indicated by the examples.

[3]Horace Silver, "Sister Sadie," copyright 1960 by Ecaroh Music.
[4]See Chapters 9 and 15 for more information on forms.

Sister Cynda

Treble Clef C Instruments
Swing

Scott Reeves

Treble Clef Instruments—Exercises for "Sister Cynda"

1. The bebop 7th scale, descending:

2. The blues scale also works well over the A section (see Chapter 8):

3. The bebop 7th scale with a chromatic passing tone, descending from the 3rd:

Sister Cynda

B♭ Instruments (saxophones play *8va*)
Swing

Scott Reeves

B♭ Instruments—Exercises for "Sister Cynda"

1. The bebop 7th scale, descending:

Sister Cynda

E♭ Instruments
Swing

Scott Reeves

E♭ Instruments—Exercises for "Sister Cynda"

1. The bebop 7th scale, descending:

2. The blues scale also works well over the A section (see Chapter 8):

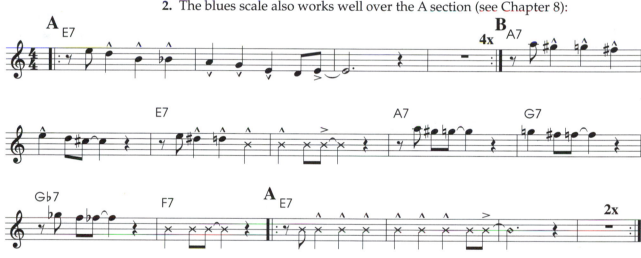

3. The bebop 7th scale with a chromatic passing tone, descending from the 3rd:

Sister Cynda

Bass Clef Instruments

Swing (play *8va* when using harmony parts)

Scott Reeves

Bass Clef Instruments—Exercises for "Sister Cynda"

1. The bebop 7th scale, descending:

2. The blues scale also works well over the A section (see Chapter 8):

3. The bebop 7th scale with a chromatic passing tone, descending from the 3rd:

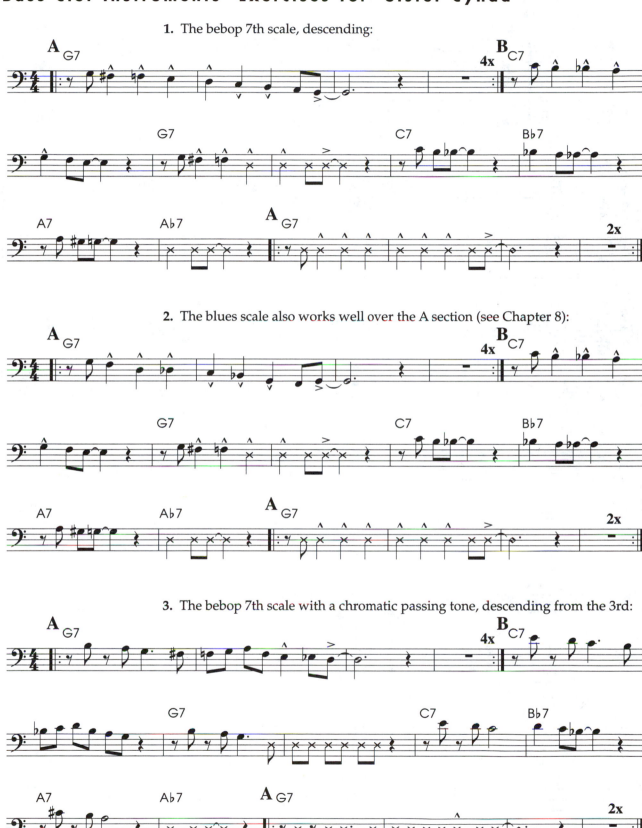

Sister Cynda

Solos (make up your own rhythms)

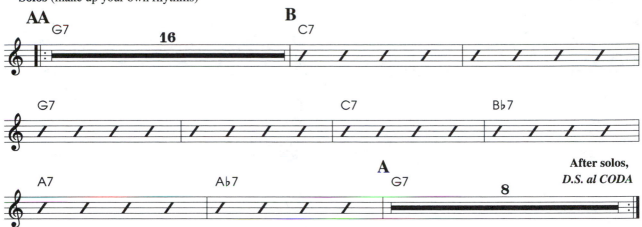

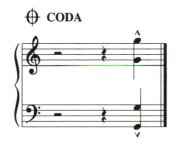

Sister Cynda

DORIAN SCALES AND MINOR 7TH CHORDS

The *dorian scale* can be thought of as a major scale with a lowered 3rd and a lowered 7th.

C Dorian Scale   C Major Scale

The dorian scale also contains the same notes as the major scale a major 2nd below.

C Dorian Scale   B♭ Major Scale

The dorian scale has a "mellow" or "blue" quality and is used when improvising over minor 7th chords, particularly when the minor chord occurs in a major key or in a *modal tune* (a song in which the chords last at least four measures). When a minor chord occurs in a minor key, the melodic minor, the harmonic minor, or the natural minor scale tends to be used in place of the dorian scale.[1]

---

[1]Refer to Chapter 10 for further information on these scales.

Minor 7th chords are made up of the first, third, fifth, and seventh notes of the dorian scale (referred to as the *root,* the *minor 3rd,* the *perfect 5th,* and the *minor 7th* of the chord).

C Minor 7th Chord

You can extend this chord by adding the second, fourth, and sixth notes of the dorian scale an octave higher. These notes are called the *major 9th,* the *perfect 11th,* and the *major 13th* of the chord, respectively.

C Minor 13th Chord

When writing the name of the chord, you need indicate only the highest chord extension. The lower numbered extensions will be assumed to be present.

Minor 7th chords have a sad, mellow, or melancholy quality. In major keys, they often progress up a 4th to a dominant chord. Songs such as John Coltrane's "Blues Minor" and "Impressions" and Miles Davis's "So What" are made up entirely of minor 7th chords.[2] Before practicing the following exercises, try singing dorian scales and playing minor 7th chords on the piano.

DORIAN SCALE WARM-UPS

Play the following exercises over the chord progression, using either a metronome, a live rhythm section, or the "Dorian and Blues Scale Warm-Ups" play-along track on the companion CD. Play the written example over the first chord; then use your ear to play the exercise in the different keys indicated by the chord symbols. You will find it helpful to look at the chord progression instead of the exercises when playing in the remaining eleven keys. Pick a tempo at which you can effortlessly play each exercise, gradually moving on to more difficult exercises after you have mastered the easier ones.

Treble Clef C Instruments—Chord Progression

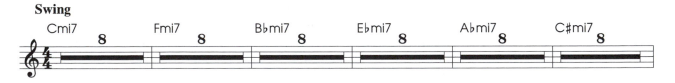

[2]The music to these songs may be found in the following volumes of *A New Approach to Jazz Improvisation:* "Blues Minor" (Vol. 27), "Impressions" (Vols. 28 and 54), and "So What" (Vol. 5).

Treble Clef C Instruments—Beginning Exercises

1. Scale fragment 1:

2. A scale fragment beginning on the fifth note of the scale. This pattern is similar to a Duke Pearson motive from "Jeannine."[3]

Treble Clef C Instruments—Intermediate Exercises

3. The dorian scale, from the root to the 5th and the 5th to the 9th:

4. The complete dorian scale to the 9th:

5. The minor 7th arpeggio:

Treble Clef C Instruments—Advanced Exercises

6. An arpeggio descending from the 11th to the 5th of the chord:

[3]Duke Pearson, "Jeannine," copyright 1960 by Upam Music Co.

7. A melodic idea descending from the 9th. This pattern is similar to a Garnett Brown motive from "Bacha Feelin'."[4]

8. A scalar idea that begins with the notes a half step below and a whole step above the root of the chord:

B♭ Instruments—Chord Progression

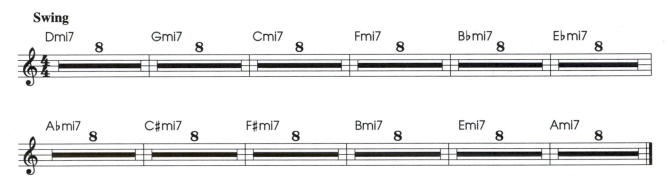

B♭ Instruments—Beginning Exercises

1. Scale fragment 1:

2. A scale fragment beginning on the fifth note of the scale. This pattern is similar to a Duke Pearson motive from "Jeannine."

[4]Garnett Brown, "Bacha Feelin'," copyright by Shelmark Publishing Co.

B♭ Instruments—Intermediate Exercises

3. The dorian scale, from the root to the 5th and the 5th to the 9th:

4. The complete dorian scale to the 9th:

5. The minor 7th arpeggio:

B♭ Instruments—Advanced Exercises

6. An arpeggio descending from the 11th to the 5th of the chord:

7. A melodic idea descending from the 9th. This pattern is similar to a Garnett Brown motive from "Bacha Feelin'."

8. A scalar idea that begins with the notes a half step below and a whole step above the root of the chord:

E♭ Instruments—Chord Progression

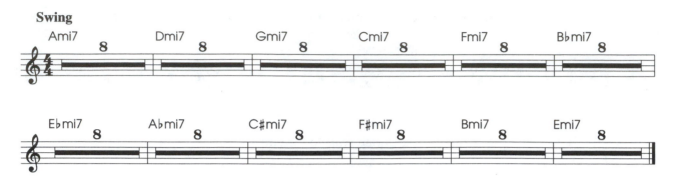

E♭ Instruments—Beginning Exercises

1. Scale fragment 1:

2. A scale fragment beginning on the fifth note of the scale. This pattern is similar to a Duke Pearson motive from "Jeannine."

E♭ Instruments—Intermediate Exercises

3. The dorian scale, from the root to the 5th and the 5th to the 9th:

4. The complete dorian scale to the 9th:

5. The minor 7th arpeggio:

E♭ Instruments—Advanced Exercises

6. An arpeggio descending from the 11th to the 5th of the chord:

7. A melodic idea descending from the 9th. This pattern is similar to a Garnett Brown motive from "Bacha Feelin'."

8. A scalar idea that begins with the notes a half step below and a whole step above the root of the chord:

Bass Clef Instruments—Chord Progression

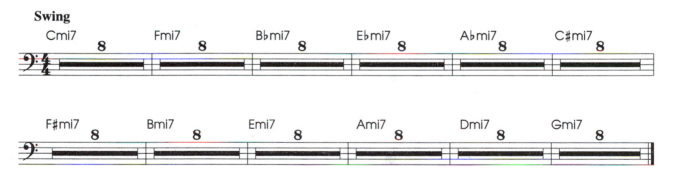

Bass Clef Instruments—Beginning Exercises

1. Scale fragment 1:

2. A scale fragment beginning on the fifth note of the scale. This pattern is similar to a Duke Pearson motive from "Jeannine."

Bass Clef Instruments—Intermediate Exercises

3. The dorian scale, from the root to the 5th and the 5th to the 9th:

4. The complete dorian scale to the 9th:

5. The minor 7th arpeggio:

Bass Clef Instruments—Advanced Exercises

6. An arpeggio descending from the 11th to the 5th of the chord:

7. A melodic idea descending from the 9th. This pattern is similar to a Garnett Brown motive from "Bacha Feelin'."

8. A scalar idea that begins with the notes a half step below and a whole step above the root of the chord:

All Instruments—Improvisation Exercises

1. Improvise on minor 7th chords in all keys, using a live rhythm section or the "Dorian and Blues Scale Warm-Ups" play-along track on the companion CD.

2. Make up your own exercises and melodic ideas based on dorian scales and minor 7th chords.

Improvising on Minor 7th Chords

"Eric's Song" is a composition based on minor 7th chords suspended over a bass note. Practice and improvise on the song, using either a metronome, a live rhythm section, or the "Eric's Song" track on the companion CD. (On the CD, the chord progression is played five times.)

"Eric's Song" has a 36-bar form in which the chords descend by half steps and whole steps. A bass line with a syncopated rhythm characterizes the first sixteen bars, whereas a strong *pedal point* anchors bars 17–24.[5] A walking bass line gives variety to bars 25–32, and time seems to "stop" during the last four bars.

Each sonority in this composition is a minor 7th chord over a bass note a perfect 5th below. When improvising, you can use the dorian scale based on the root of the minor 7th chord or the mixolydian or bebop 7th scale based on the bass note. The dorian and mixolydian choices for each chord contain the same notes, but thinking in terms of each scale may suggest different types of melodies. The scales in concert pitch are as follows:

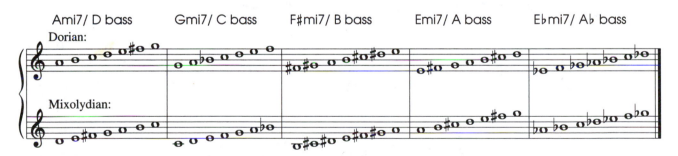

Before improvising on the composition, practice the chord progression by outlining the chords with the exercises that follow the song.

[5]A pedal point is a continuously repeated tone.

Eric's Song

Treble Clef C Instruments
Latin

Scott Reeves

Solos on the form, using the chord symbols above the melody.
After solos, *D.C. al CODA*

Treble Clef Instruments—Exercises for "Eric's Song"

1. Play Mixolydian and Bebop 7th Scale Warm-Ups 2, 3, 4, 6, and 7 (Chapter 5) based on the bass note of each bitonal chord in the progression. Play the exercise twice over the chords lasting eight bars and once over the final chord.

   a. Mixolydian and Bebop 7th Scale Warm-Up 3:

2. Play Dorian Scale Warm-Ups 2, 3, 4, 6, 7, and 8 based on the minor 7th chords in the progression. Play the exercise twice over the chords lasting eight bars and once over the final chord.

   a. Dorian Scale Warm-Up 6:

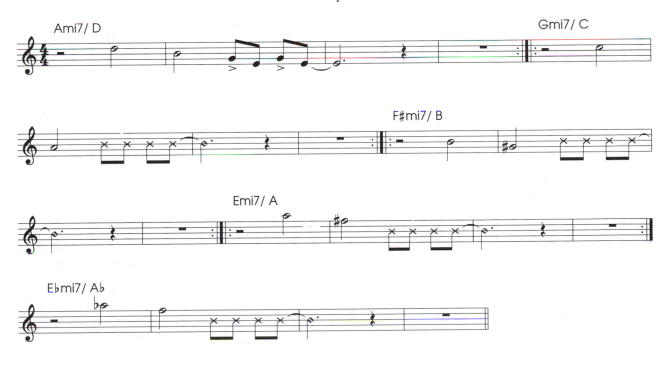

Eric's Song

Bb Instruments
Latin

Scott Reeves

Solos on the form, using the chord
symbols above the melody.
After solos, *D.C. al CODA*

B♭ Instruments—Exercises for "Eric's Song"

1. Play Mixolydian and Bebop 7th Scale Warm-Ups 2, 3, 4, 6, and 7 (Chapter 5) based on the bass note of each bitonal chord in the progression. Play the exercise twice over the chords lasting eight bars and once over the final chord.

   a. Mixolydian and Bebop 7th Scale Warm-Up 3:

2. Play Dorian Scale Warm-Ups 2, 3, 4, 6, 7, and 8 based on the minor 7th chords in the progression. Play the exercise twice over the chords lasting eight bars and once over the final chord.

   a. Dorian Scale Warm-Up 6:

Eric's Song

E♭ **Instruments**

Scott Reeves

Solos on the form, using the chord
symbols above the melody.

After solos, *D.C. al CODA*

E♭ Instruments—Exercises for "Eric's Song"

1. Play Mixolydian and Bebop 7th Scale Warm-Ups 2, 3, 4, 6, and 7 (Chapter 5) based on the bass note of each bitonal chord in the progression. Play the exercise twice over the chords lasting eight bars and once over the final chord.

   a. Mixolydian and Bebop 7th Scale Warm-Up 3:

2. Play Dorian Scale Warm-Ups 2, 3, 4, 6, 7, and 8 based on the minor 7th chords in the progression. Play the exercise twice over the chords lasting eight bars and once over the final chord.

   a. Dorian Scale Warm-Up 6:

Eric's Song

Solos on the form, using the chord symbols above the melody.
After solos, *D.C. al CODA*

Bass Clef Instruments—Exercises for "Eric's Song"

1. Play Mixolydian and Bebop 7th Scale Warm-Ups 2, 3, 4, 6, and 7 (Chapter 5) based on the bass note of each bitonal chord in the progression. Play the exercise twice over the chords lasting eight bars and once over the final chord.

   a. Mixolydian and Bebop 7th Scale Warm-Up 3:

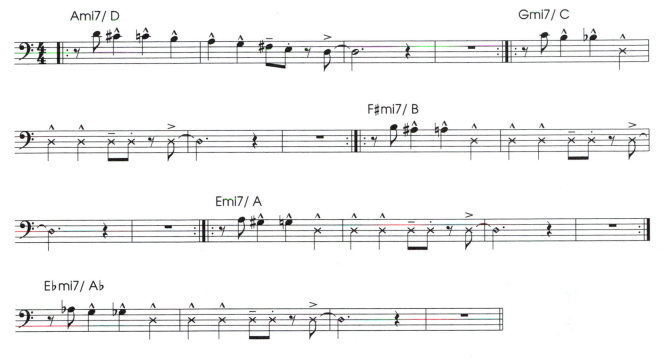

2. Play Dorian Scale Warm-Ups 2, 3, 4, 6, 7, and 8 based on the minor 7th chords in the progression. Play the exercise twice over the chords lasting eight bars and once over the final chord.

   a. Dorian Scale Warm-Up 6:

Eric's Song

Piano/Guitar
Latin

Scott Reeves

Repeat for solos. After all solos,
D.C. al CODA

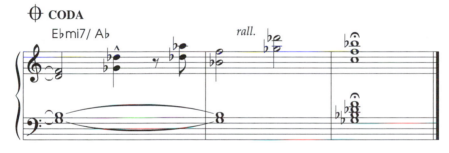

Eric's Song

THE ii–V–I PROGRESSION

Minor 7th, dominant 7th, and major 7th chords often occur in succession as part of a chord progression. When that happens, the minor 7th chord typically moves up a perfect 4th to the dominant 7th chord, which in turn progresses down a perfect 5th to the major 7th chord.

The ii–V–I Progression in C Major

This sequence of chords is called the ii–V–I progression because the minor 7th, dominant 7th, and major 7th chords are built on the second, fifth, and first notes of the major scale. Lowercase roman numerals are used to denote minor 7th chords, and uppercase roman numerals are used for dominant 7th and major 7th chords. The first, second, and fifth notes of any scale are also referred to as the *tonic*, the *supertonic*, and the *dominant*, respectively.

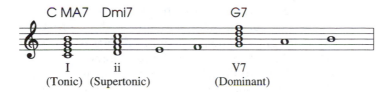

Often, only a portion of this sequence occurs, in the form of either a ii–V or a V–I chord progression.

The ii–V Progression   The V–I Progression

Another variation involves the use of the minor chord built on the sixth note of the major scale, creating a I–vi–ii–V–I progression. The minor vi and minor ii chords can also be changed to dominant 7th chords; this permutation is sometimes referred to as a I–VI–II–V–I progression but is more correctly described as a I–V-of-ii–V-of-V–V–I progression.[1]

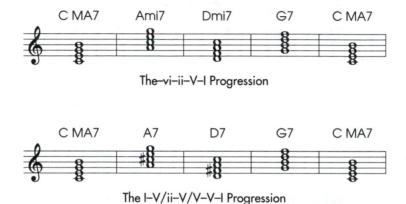

The–vi–ii–V–I Progression

The I–V/ii–V/V–V–I Progression

As we learned in the preceding chapters, the minor 7th chord is colored by the dorian scale, the dominant 7th chord by the mixolydian scale, and the major 7th chord by the major scale.

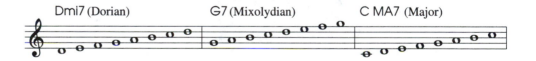

When we compare these three scales, we notice that they all contain the same notes. Therefore, whenever we find a ii–V–I progression, we can view all three chords as being in one key. Although you may wish to stress different notes in each chord (such as the 3rds and the 7ths), one scale will essentially color all three chords, greatly simplifying the process of improvisation.

As you become familiar with this chord progression, you will notice that it occurs with great frequency. "All the Things You Are," "Cherokee," "Confirmation," "Donna Lee," "Four," "Giant Steps," "Groovin' High," "I'll Remember April," "Joy Spring," "Lady Bird," "Moment's Notice," "Ornithology," "Peace," "Pent-Up House," "Perdido," "Satin Doll," "Scrapple from the Apple," "Take the 'A' Train,"

---

[1]Dominant 7th chords that substitute for other chords are called secondary dominants. Refer to Chapter 15 for more information on these chords.

and "Tune-Up" are among the many tunes that use ii–V–I progressions.[2] Develop your ability to recognize this progression by playing the chords on the piano.

ii–V–I PROGRESSION WARM-UPS

Play the following exercises over the chord progression, using either a metronome, a live rhythm section, or the "ii–V–I Progression and Diminished Scale Warm-Ups" play-along track on the companion CD. Play the written example over the first chord; then use your ear to play the exercise in the different keys indicated by the chord symbols. You will find it helpful to look at the chord progression instead of the exercises when playing in the remaining eleven keys. Pick a tempo at which you can effortlessly play each exercise, gradually moving on to more difficult exercises after you have mastered the easier ones.

Treble Clef C Instruments—Chord Progression

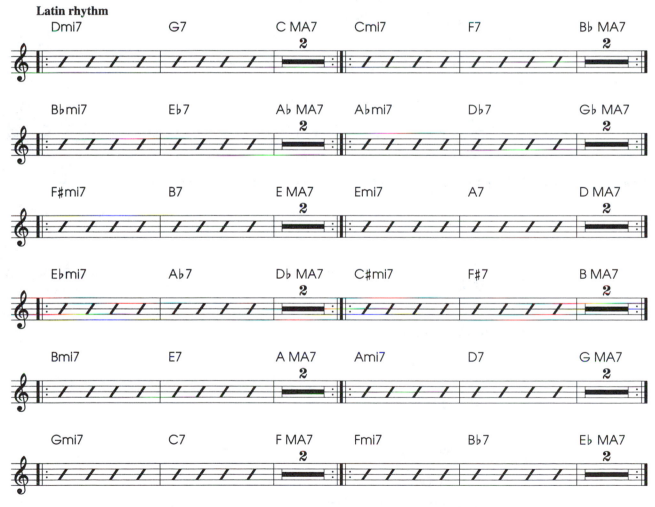

[2]The music to these songs may be found in the following volumes of *A New Approach to Jazz Improvisation:* "All the Things You Are" (Vol. 43), "Cherokee" (Vol. 15), "Confirmation" (Vol. 6), "Donna Lee" (Vol. 6), "Four" (Vol. 7), "Giant Steps" (Vol. 28), "Goovin' High" (Vol. 43), "I'll Remember April" (Vol. 43), "Joy Spring" (Vol. 53), "Lady Bird" (Vol. 36), "Moment's Notice" (Vol. 38), "Ornithology" (Vol. 6), "Peace" (Vol. 17), "Pent-Up House" (Vol. 8), "Perdido" (Vol. 12), "Satin Doll" (Vols. 12 and 54), "Scrapple from the Apple" (Vol. 6), "Take the 'A' Train" (Vol. 12), "Tune-Up" (Vol. 7).

Treble Clef C Instruments—Beginning Exercises

1. A *guide-tone line* is a melody that starts on the 3rd or the 7th of a chord and moves to the 3rd or the 7th of the following chord, whichever is closer. The following guide-tone line starts on the 7th of the ii chord, moves to the 3rd of the V chord, and resolves to the 7th of the I chord. Syncopated rhythms as well as other scale tones are added for melodic interest.

2. A guide-tone line that begins on the 3rd of the ii chord, moves to the 7th of the V chord, and resolves to the 3rd of the I chord:

3. Using the dorian scale over all three chords in the progression:

Treble Clef C Instruments—Intermediate Exercises

4. Using the bebop 7th scale over all three chords in the progression:

5. Using the major scale over all three chords in the progression:

6. A melodic pattern based on the dorian scale:

Treble Clef C Instruments—Advanced Exercises

7. Arpeggios starting on the root of the ii chord and the 3rd of the V chord:

8. A pattern starting on the 5th of the ii chord that uses both the major and the minor 7th over the V chord:

B♭ Instruments—Chord Progression

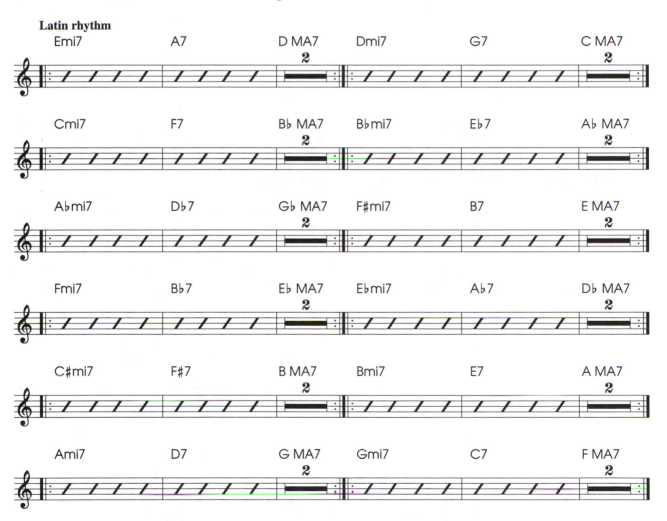

B♭ Instruments—Beginning Exercises

1. A *guide-tone line* is a melody that starts on the 3rd or the 7th of a chord and moves to the 3rd or the 7th of the following chord, whichever is closer. The following guide-tone line starts on the 7th of the ii chord, moves to the 3rd of the V chord, and resolves to the 7th of the I chord. Syncopated rhythms as well as other scale tones are added for melodic interest.

2. A guide-tone line that begins on the 3rd of the ii chord, moves to the 7th of the V chord, and resolves to the 3rd of the I chord:

3. Using the dorian scale over all three chords in the progression:

B♭ Instruments—Intermediate Exercises

4. Using the bebop 7th scale over all three chords in the progression:

5. Using the major scale over all three chords in the progression:

6. A melodic pattern based on the dorian scale:

B♭ Instruments—Advanced Exercises

7. Arpeggios starting on the root of the ii chord and the 3rd of the V chord:

8. A pattern starting on the 5th of the ii chord that uses both the major and the minor 7th over the V chord:

E♭ Instruments—Chord Progression

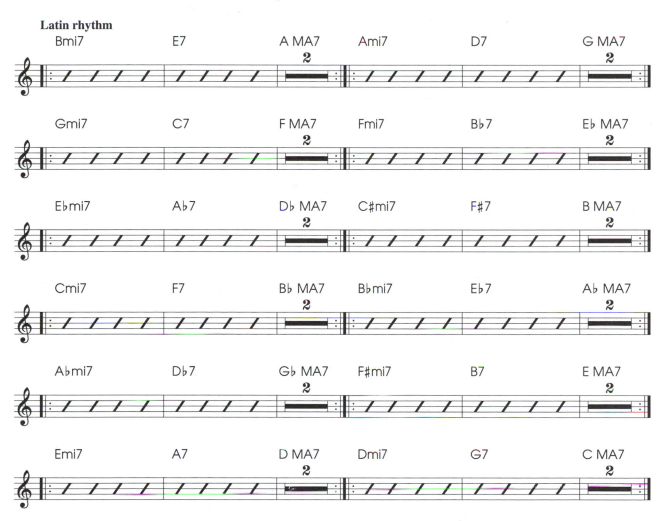

E♭ Instruments—Beginning Exercises

1. A *guide-tone line* is a melody that starts on the 3rd or the 7th of a chord and moves to the 3rd or the 7th of the following chord, whichever is closer. The following guide-tone line starts on the 7th of the ii chord, moves to the 3rd of the V chord, and resolves to the 7th of the I chord. Syncopated rhythms as well as other scale tones are added for melodic interest.

2. A guide-tone line that begins on the 3rd of the ii chord, moves to the 7th of the V chord, and resolves to the 3rd of the I chord:

3. Using the dorian scale over all three chords in the progression:

E♭ Instruments—Intermediate Exercises

4. Using the bebop 7th scale over all three chords in the progression:

5. Using the major scale over all three chords in the progression:

6. A melodic pattern based on the dorian scale:

E♭ Instruments—Advanced Exercises

7. Arpeggios starting on the root of the ii chord and the 3rd of the V chord:

8. A pattern starting on the 5th of the ii chord that uses both the major and the minor 7th over the V chord:

Bass Clef Instruments—Chord Progression

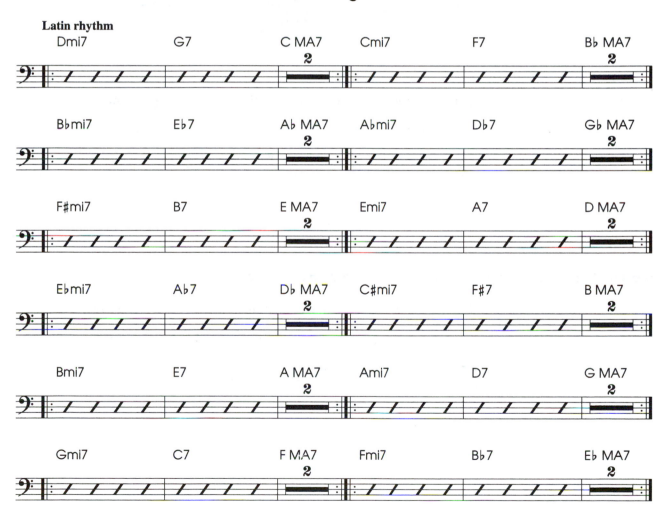

Bass Clef Instruments—Beginning Exercises

1. A *guide-tone line* is a melody that starts on the 3rd or the 7th of a chord and moves to the 3rd or the 7th of the following chord, whichever is closer. The following guide-tone line starts on the 7th of the ii chord, moves to the 3rd of the V chord, and resolves to the 7th of the I chord. Syncopated rhythms as well as other scale tones are added for melodic interest.

2. A guide-tone line that begins on the 3rd of the ii chord, moves to the 7th of the V chord, and resolves to the 3rd of the I chord:

3. Using the dorian scale over all three chords in the progression:

Bass Clef Instruments—Intermediate Exercises

4. Using the bebop 7th scale over all three chords in the progression:

5. Using the major scale over all three chords in the progression:

6. A melodic pattern based on the dorian scale:

Bass Clef Instruments—Advanced Exercises

7. Arpeggios starting on the root of the ii chord and the 3rd of the V chord:

8. A pattern starting on the 5th of the ii chord that uses both the major and the minor 7th over the V chord:

All Instruments—Improvisation Exercises

1. Improvise on ii–V–I progressions in all keys, using a live rhythm section or the "ii–V–I Progression and Diminished Scale Warm-Ups" play-along track on the companion CD.

2. Make up your own exercises and melodic ideas based on ii–V–I progressions.

ℐMPROVISING ON ii–V–I PROGRESSIONS

"The Countess" is a composition that contains numerous ii–V and ii–V–I progressions. Practice and improvise on the song, using either a metronome, a live rhythm section, or the "Countess" play-along track on the companion CD. (On the CD, the chord progression is played four times.)

"The Countess" is based on the chord progression to the Ellington-Strayhorn standard "Satin Doll."[3] Like "Sister Cynda," it has a 32-bar AABA form. The A section begins with a ii–V progression in the key of C major concert, followed by three more ii–V progressions, whose purpose is to depart from and return to the chord of resolution—C major 7. The concert D♭7 chord in the sixth bar is known as a *tritone substitution* and serves as a replacement for the concert G7 chord (the dominant 7th chord a tritone away).[4]

The B section begins with a ii–V–I progression in F concert, followed by a ii–V–I progression in G concert, although the final chord of that progression is G7, not G major 7.

After playing the melody, practice the chord progression by outlining the chords with the exercises that follow the song.

---

[3]Billy Strayhorn, Duke Ellington, and Johnny Mercer, "Satin Doll," copyright 1958 by Tempo Music.

[4]Refer to Chapter 15 for more information on the tritone substitution.

The Countess

Treble Clef C Instruments

Swing

Scott Reeves

Treble Clef Instruments—Exercises for "The Countess"

1. Play a guide-tone line over the chord progression, with each note lasting the duration of the chord. Start with the 3rd or the 7th of the first chord, and move to the 7th or the 3rd of the following chord, whichever is closer.

2. Outlining the chords with dorian and major scales:

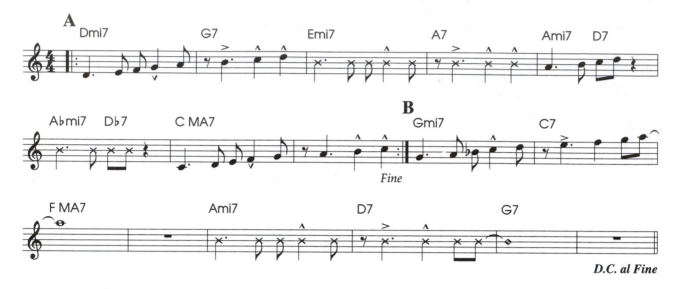

3. Outlining the chords with bebop 7th and major scales:

4. Arpeggios starting on the root of the ii chord and the 3rd of the V chord:

Fine

D.C. al Fine

The Countess

B♭ Instruments—Exercises for "The Countess"

1. Play a guide-tone line over the chord progression, with each note lasting the duration of the chord. Start with the 3rd or the 7th of the first chord, and move to the 7th or the 3rd of the following chord, whichever is closer.

2. Outlining the chords with dorian and major scales:

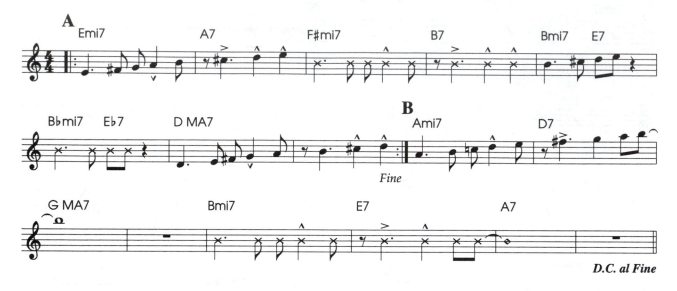

3. Outlining the chords with bebop 7th and major scales:

4. Arpeggios starting on the root of the ii chord and the 3rd of the V chord:

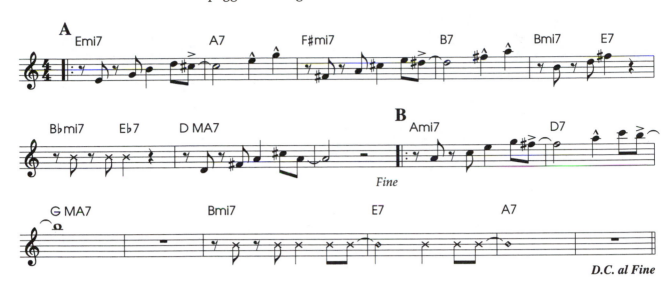

The Countess

Scott Reeves

Eb Instruments
Swing

E♭ Instruments—Exercises for "The Countess"

1. Play a guide-tone line over the chord progression, with each note lasting the duration of the chord. Start with the 3rd or the 7th of the first chord, and move to the 7th or the 3rd of the following chord, whichever is closer.

2. Outlining the chords with dorian and major scales:

3. Outlining the chords with bebop 7th and major scales:

4. Arpeggios starting on the root of the ii chord and the 3rd of the V chord:

The Countess

Bass Clef Instruments
Swing

Scott Reeves

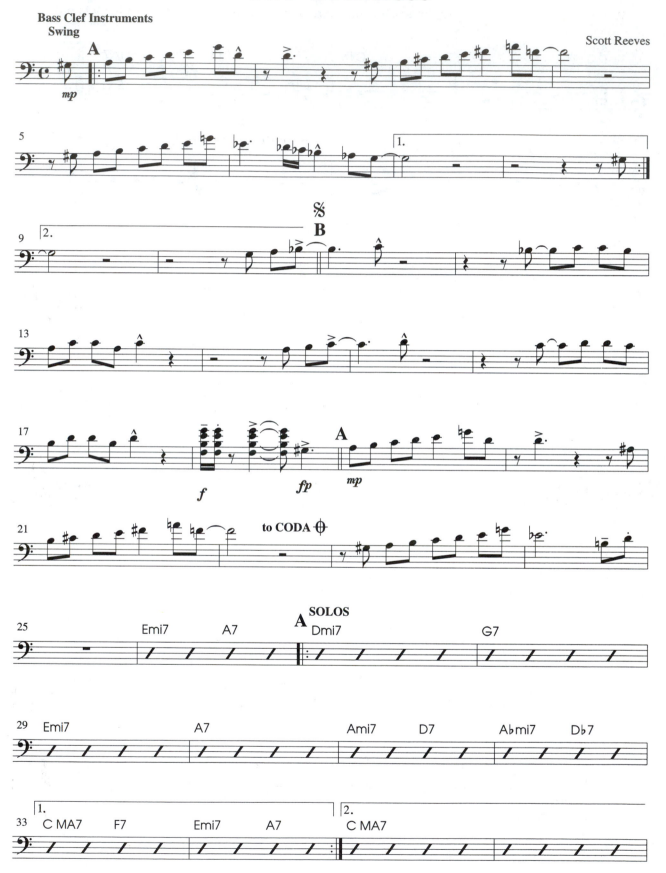

Bass Clef Instruments—Exercises for "The Countess"

1. Play a guide-tone line over the chord progression, with each note lasting the duration of the chord. Start with the 3rd or the 7th of the first chord, and move to the 7th or the 3rd of the following chord, whichever is closer.

2. Outlining the chords with dorian and major scales:

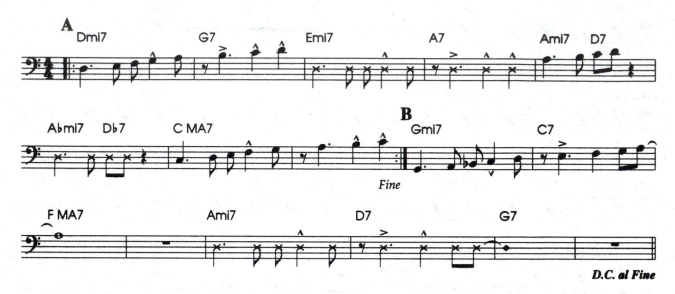

3. Outlining the chords with bebop 7th and major scales:

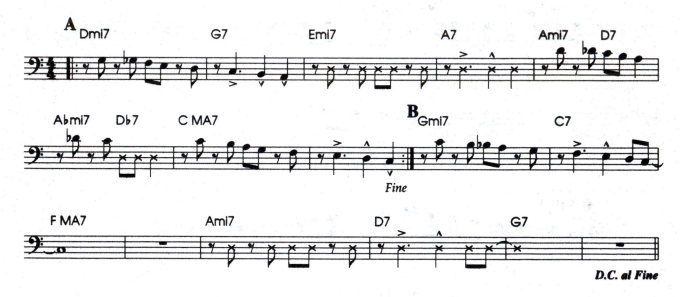

4. Arpeggios starting on the root of the ii chord and the 3rd of the V chord:

D.C. al Fine

The Countess

Piano/ Guitar
Swing

Scott Reeves

Repeat for solos. After all solos,
D.C. al CODA

The Countess

Bass
Swing

Scott Reeves

When we play this music we see people smile and feel happy. And that's a tremendous feeling . . . to heal people with music. Jazz, you feel good if you listen to it, you feel good if you play it. You feel good if you write it.

—pianist Randy Weston

CHAPTER

8

THE BLUES FORM AND THE BLUES SCALE

The word "blues" has at least three different connotations: a feeling, a musical style, and a form. When we describe a song as being "bluesy," we are referring to its feeling or mood. This bluesy quality is usually due to the song's being in a minor key or to the performer's use of the blues scale and *blue* or *bent notes*. The latter are notes that fall between the pitches on the piano, typically between the ♭3rd and the 3rd and between the ♭5 and the 5th notes of the scale. The blues feeling can be applied to many types of tunes, including those songs not cast in the blues form.

The musical genre called the *blues* is a style of music that originated in the rural South in the early 1900s with African-American performers such as Huddie "Leadbelly" Ledbetter and Robert Johnson. It soon evolved into a popular form of entertainment in cities such as Memphis. Singers Ma Rainey and Bessie Smith and composer W. C. Handy are synonymous with this *urban blues* style. The blues then migrated to Chicago and other Northern American cities and is carried on by performers such as B. B. King, Muddy Waters, and Howling Wolf. It also influenced a diversity of rock musicians, including Elvis Presley, Bonnie Raitt, and Eric Clapton.

Urban blues songs are usually written in the blues form, but jazz and other contemporary styles of music also employ this form. The *blues form* is a 12-measure structure consisting of three phrases of four measures each, often occurring in a question-question-answer format.

| *Question/Statement* | *Question/Statement* | *Answer/Response* |
| 4 | 4 | 4 |

The Blues Form

Many chord progressions have been applied to this form. The simplest uses three dominant 7th chords.

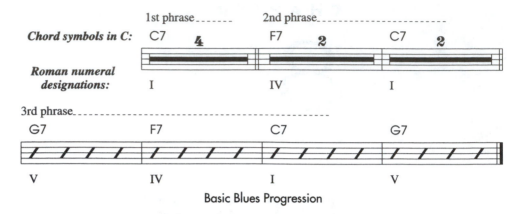

Basic Blues Progression

Later on, ii–V–I progressions were added during the third phrase:

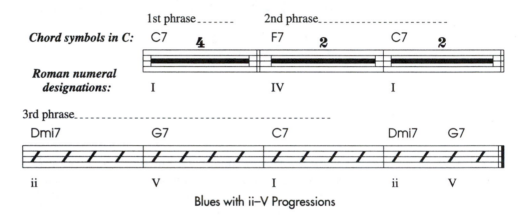

Blues with ii–V Progressions

The blues form is also found in a minor key.

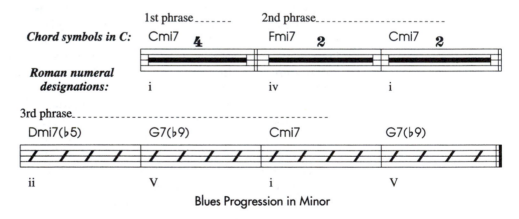

Blues Progression in Minor

Since the 1940s, there have been many variations involving chord substitutions and extensions to the length of the 12-measure form. The following is an example of a blues in a major key with numerous substitutions. For further information on ways to vary the blues progression, refer to *Creative Jazz Improvisation*.[1]

[1]Scott D. Reeves, *Creative Jazz Improvisation*, 2nd ed. (Englewood Cliffs, N.J.: Prentice Hall, 1995), pp. 102–108.

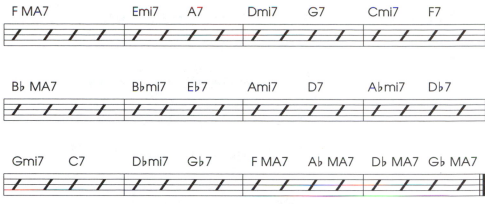

Blues Progression in Major with Chord Substitutions

The blues is perhaps the most commonly used form in jazz, with thousands of compositions utilizing some variation of this 12-measure format. Some well-known blues tunes include "All Blues," "Billie's Bounce," "Blue Trane," "C Jam Blues," "Freddie Freeloader," "Mr. P.C.," "Now's the Time," "Tenor Madness," and "Watermelon Man."[2]

The *blues scale* is a six-note scale consisting of a minor 3rd, a whole step, a half step, a half step, a minor 3rd, and a whole step.

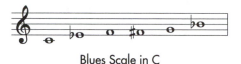

Blues Scale in C

It is used to improvise over dominant 7th and minor 7th chords, not only within the blues form, but in many other types of songs as well. The ♭3rd of the scale rubbing against the major 3rd of the dominant chord, as well as the clash of the ♯4 against the 5th, gives this scale its characteristic "bluesy" sound. These notes are often "bent," creating "blue notes" between the normal pitches. The blues scale is found in styles as diverse as early blues, jazz, rock, gospel, Motown, and contemporary pop music, whenever a "soulful" sound is called for.

BLUES SCALE WARM-UPS

Play the following exercises over the chord progression, using either a metronome, a live rhythm section, or the "Dorian and Blues Scale Warm-Ups" play-along track on the companion CD. Play the written example over the first chord; then use your ear to play the exercise in the different keys indicated by the chord symbols. You will find it helpful to look at the chord progression instead of the exercises when playing in the remaining eleven keys. Pick a tempo at which you can effortlessly play each exercise, gradually moving on to more difficult exercises after you have mastered the easier ones.

[2]The music to these songs may be found in the following volumes of *A New Approach to Jazz Improvisation:* "All Blues" (Vol. 50), "Billie's Bounce" (Vol. 6), "Blue Trane" (Vol. 38), "C Jam Blues" (Vol. 48), "Freddie Freeloader" (Vol. 50), "Mr. P. C." (Vol. 27), "Now's the Time" (Vol. 6), "Tenor Madness" (Vol. 8), "Watermelon Man" (Vols. 11 and 54).

Treble Clef C Instruments—Chord Progression

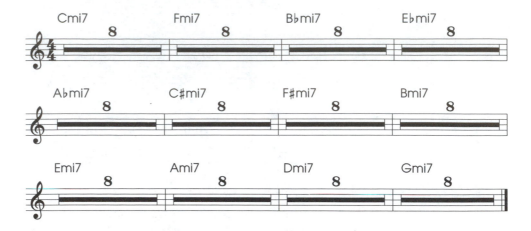

Treble Clef C Instruments—Beginning Exercises

1. Blues riff 1:

2. Blues riff 2:

Treble Clef C Instruments—Intermediate Exercises

3. The blues scale, ascending:

4. The blues scale, descending. This pattern is similar to "Sonnymoon for Two" by Sonny Rollins.[3]

[3]Sonny Rollins, "Sonnymoon for Two," copyright by Blue Horizon Music, BMI.

5. A paraphrase of the opening motive of Dizzy Gillespie's composition "Birk's Works."[4] This pattern anticipates each chord change by three eighth notes.

Treble Clef C Instruments—Advanced Exercises

6. A descending blues pattern, similar to the song "S.K.J." by Milt Jackson:[5]

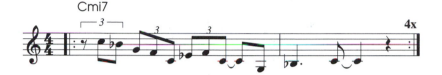

7. A blues riff in triplets that begins on a blue note:

B♭ Instruments—Chord Progression

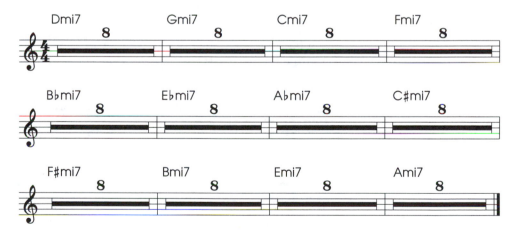

---

[4]Dizzy Gillespie, "Birk's Works," copyright by Iwo Music, ASCAP.
[5]Milt Jackson, "S.K.J.," copyright by Reccie Music, BMI.

B♭ Instruments—Beginning Exercises

1. Blues riff 1:

2. Blues riff 2:

B♭ Instruments—Intermediate Exercises

3. The blues scale, ascending:

4. The blues scale, descending. This pattern is similar to "Sonnymoon for Two" by Sonny Rollins.

5. A paraphrase of the opening motive of Dizzy Gillespie's composition "Birk's Works." This pattern anticipates each chord change by three eighth notes.

B♭ Instruments—Advanced Exercises

6. A descending blues pattern, similar to the song "S.K.J." by Milt Jackson:

7. A blues riff in triplets that begins on a blue note:

E♭ Instruments—Chord Progression

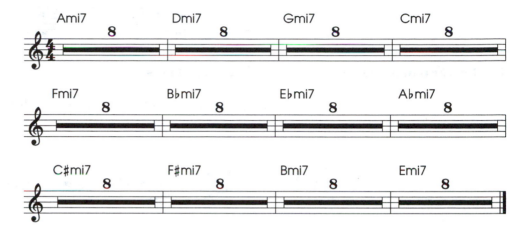

E♭ Instruments—Beginning Exercises

1. Blues riff 1:

2. Blues riff 2:

E♭ Instruments—Intermediate Exercises

3. The blues scale, ascending:

4. The blues scale, descending. This pattern is similar to "Sonnymoon for Two" by Sonny Rollins.

5. A paraphrase of the opening motive of Dizzy Gillespie's composition "Birk's Works." This pattern anticipates each chord change by three eighth notes.

Eb Instruments—Advanced Exercises

6. A descending blues pattern, similar to the song "S.K.J." by Milt Jackson:

7. A blues riff in triplets that begins on a blue note:

Bass Clef Instruments—Chord Progression

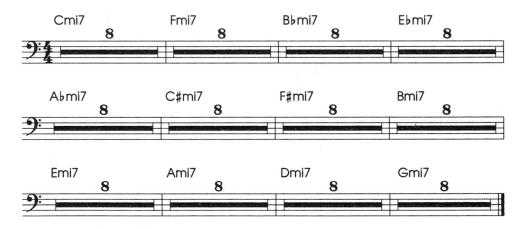

Bass Clef Instruments—Beginning Exercises

1. Blues riff 1:

2. Blues riff 2:

Bass Clef Instruments—Intermediate Exercises

3. The blues scale, ascending:

4. The blues scale, descending. This pattern is similar to "Sonnymoon for Two" by Sonny Rollins.

5. A paraphrase of the opening motive of Dizzy Gillespie's composition "Birk's Works." This pattern anticipates each chord change by three eighth notes.

Bass Clef Instruments—Advanced Exercises

6. A descending blues pattern, similar to the song "S.K.J." by Milt Jackson:

7. A blues riff in triplets that begins on a blue note:

All Instruments—Improvisation Exercises

1. Improvise on the blues scales in twelve keys, using a live rhythm section or the "Dorian and Blues Scale Warm-Ups" play-along track on the companion CD.

2. Improvise on the blues progression in B♭ concert, using a live rhythm section or the "Rhythm Warm-Ups: Swing Rhythms" play-along track on the companion CD.

3. Make up your own exercises and melodic ideas based on blues scales and the blues form.

*J*MPROVISING ON THE BLUES FORM

"Eta Carina Blue" is a composition based on the blues form. Practice and improvise on the song, using either a metronome, a live rhythm section, or the "Eta Carina Blue" play-along track on the companion CD. (On the CD, the chord progression is played sixteen times.)

After playing the melody, practice the chord progression by outlining the chords with the exercises that follow the song. As the exercises demonstrate, you may improvise on "Eta Carina Blue" either by using one blues scale throughout or by employing the bebop 7th scales that accompany the I, IV, and V chords.

Eta Carina Blue

Treble Clef C Instruments
Swing

Scott Reeves

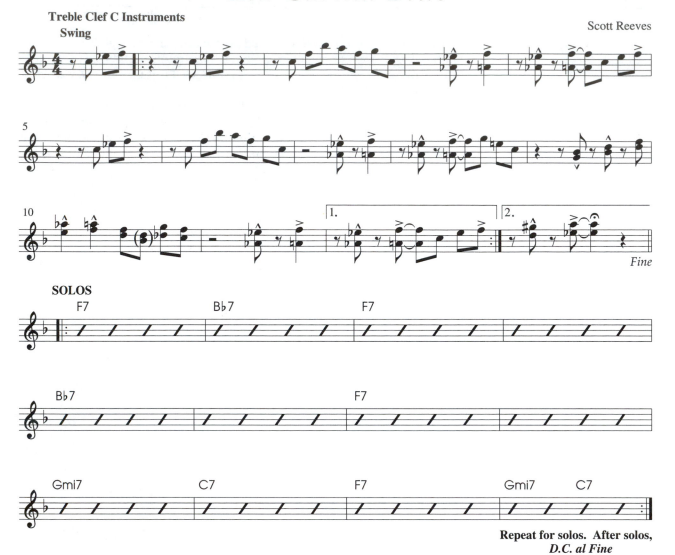

Fine

Repeat for solos. After solos,
D.C. al Fine

Treble Clef Instruments—Exercises for "Eta Carina Blue"

1–5. Play Blues Scale Warm-Ups 1, 2, and 3 six times and 4 and 5 three times, in the key of F, over the chord progression to "Eta Carina Blue."

6. The blues scale, descending in eighth notes:

7. The blues scale, ascending and descending in eighth notes:

8. Outlining the dominant 7th chords with bebop 7th scales:

Eta Carina Blue

Bb Instruments (saxophones play *8va*)
Swing

Scott Reeves

SOLOS

Repeat for solos. After solos,
D.C. al Fine

B♭ Instruments—Exercises for "Eta Carina Blue"

1–5. Play Blues Scale Warm-Ups 1, 2, and 3 six times and 4 and 5 three times, in the key of G, over the chord progression to "Eta Carina Blue."

6. The blues scale, descending in eighth notes:

7. The blues scale, ascending and descending in eighth notes:

(trumpet—*8va basso*)

8. Outlining the dominant 7th chords with bebop 7th scales:

Eta Carina Blue

E♭ Instruments
Swing

Scott Reeves

Repeat for solos. After solos,
D.C. al Fine

E♭ Instruments—Exercises for "Eta Carina Blue"

1–5. Play Blues Scale Warm-Ups 1, 2, and 3 six times and 4 and 5 three times, in the key of D, over the chord progression to "Eta Carina Blue."

6. The blues scale, descending in eighth notes:

7. The blues scale, ascending and descending in eighth notes:

8. Outlining the dominant 7th chords with bebop 7th scales:

Eta Carina Blue

Bass Clef Instruments (opt. *8va*)

Scott Reeves

Bass Clef Instruments—Exercises for "Eta Carina Blue"

1–5. Play Blues Scale Warm-Ups 1, 2, and 3 six times and 4 and 5 three times, in the key of F, over the chord progression to "Eta Carina Blue."

6. The blues scale, descending in eighth notes:

7. The blues scale, ascending and descending in eighth notes:

(opt. *8va*)

8. Outlining the dominant 7th chords with bebop 7th scales:

Eta Carina Blue

Eta Carina Blue

Scott Reeves

CHAPTER
9

SECTIONAL FORMS AND RHYTHM CHANGES

Most jazz compositions are based either on the blues form or on *sectional forms.* Sectional forms consist of complete melodic ideas called *phrases,* which occur in a given sequence. These phrases are typically eight measures long, but they are also found in other lengths, particularly four- and sixteen-measure varieties.[1]

Sectional forms come in three versions: *binary, ternary,* and *through-composed.* When these forms are analyzed, each new phrase or section is assigned a letter. If the phrases occur in an AB-AB or AB-AC sequence, the form is called binary, because the second half of the song mirrors the first. If the phrases occur in an AAB-A format, the form is called ternary, since it divides into three parts. (In ternary form, the B section is often referred to as the *bridge* or the *release.*) Most songs based on sectional forms use either the binary or the ternary format, but occasionally we find songs in which none of the phrases repeats. These are called through-composed forms.

Sometimes, jazz composers not only model their composition on one of these forms but also "borrow" the chord progression from another song, particularly popular "standards" from the 1920s and 1930s. (Melodies can receive copyright protection, but chord progressions cannot.) Compositions based on preexisting chord progressions, sometimes called *contrafacts,* became commonplace during the bebop period of the 1940s.[2] The chord progression most often "appropriated" was derived from a George Gershwin song, *"I Got Rhythm." Rhythm changes,* as they are commonly called, are based on a 32-measure AABA ternary form. The A section consists of a simple progression in the tonic key; the B section starts on the

---

[1]Scott D. Reeves, *Creative Jazz Improvisation,* 2nd ed. (Englewood Cliffs, N.J.: Prentice Hall, 1995), p. 124.

[2]The term "contrafact" was coined by Professor David Baker of Indiana University.

dominant 7th chord a major 3rd above the tonic, and returns to the original key by means of dominant 7th chords moving upward by perfect 4ths.

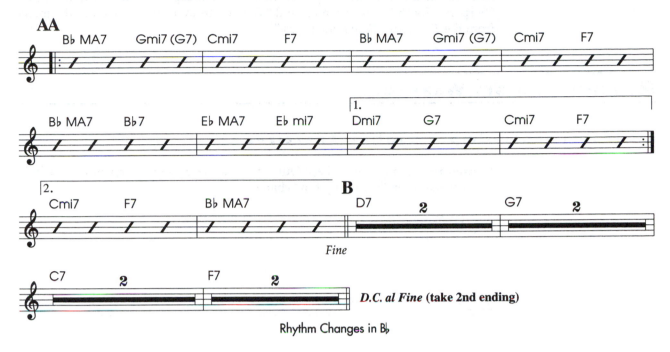

Rhythm Changes in B♭

Some of the more popular variations on this progression include the following chord substitutions:[3]

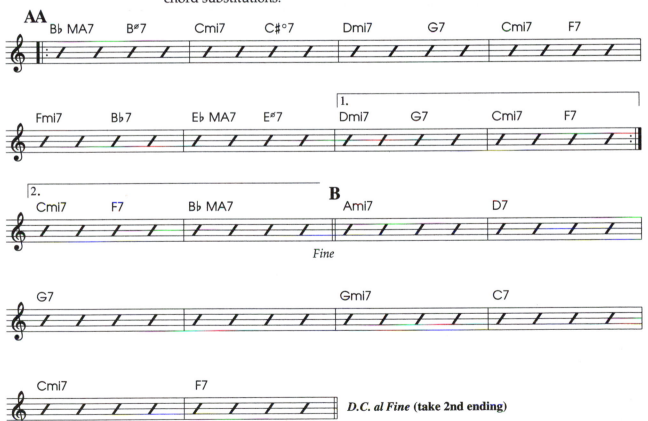

---

[3]The chords found in the second half of measures 1, 2, and 6 are types of diminished chords and will be discussed in Chapters 11 and 13.

Songs based on rhythm changes are second in popularity only to the blues. Some of the most commonly played tunes using this progression include "Oleo," "Serpents Tooth," "The Theme," and "Thrivin' from a Riff," as well as the theme from the T.V. show "The Flintstones."[4]

RHYTHM CHANGES WARM-UPS

All Instruments—Improvisation Exercises

1. After practicing "Lester Lept Out," make up your own exercises and melodic ideas based on "I Got Rhythm" changes.

[4]The music to these songs may be found in the following volumes of *A New Approach to Jazz Improvisation:* "Oleo" (Vol. 8), "Serpents Tooth" (Vol. 7), "The Theme" (Vol. 7), "Thrivin' from a Riff" (Vol. 6).

♩MPROVISING ON RHYTHM CHANGES

"Lester Lept Out" is a composition based on the chord changes to "I Got Rhythm."[5] Practice and improvise on the song, using either a metronome, a live rhythm section, or the "Lester Lept Out" play-along track on the companion CD. (On the CD, the chord progression is played six times.)

The A section of "Lester Lept Out" contains a simple rhythmic idea called a *riff*. The B section is based on a motive played by the great tenor saxophonist Lester Young during his improvisation on his composition "Lester Leaps In."[6]

Jazz musicians have traditionally gravitated toward "I Got Rhythm" changes in part because of the possibilities inherent in the chords to the A section. The various chords have so many notes in common that it is possible to color the entire A section with one major scale, one blues scale, or one major pentatonic scale, although not every note will perfectly fit each chord.[7] Conversely, the improvisor can choose to emphasize the notes that are not common to all the chords, typically the 3rds and the 7ths of each chord, to bring out the sound of each individual chord change. The exercises that follow the song illustrate the difference between these two approaches, as will a comparison of Lester Young's solo on "Lester Leaps In" with Charlie Parker's solo on "Shaw 'Nuff" from *Creative Jazz Improvisation*.[8]

---

[5]George Gershwin, "I Got Rhythm," copyright 1930, renewed by WB Music Corp.
[6]Reeves, *Creative Jazz Improvisation*, p. 46.
[7]Refer to Chapter 12 for more information on pentatonic scales.
[8]Reeves, *Creative Jazz Improvisation*, pp. 45–52, 133–138.

Lester Lept Out

Treble Clef C Instruments

Swing

Scott Reeves

**Solos on the form (AABA); use the chord symbols
above the melody for your improvisation.**

Fine

Treble Clef Instruments—Exercises for "Lester Lept Out"

1. A guide-tone line that brings out the sound of each chord. After practicing and memorizing the line, improvise a solo based on these pitches, using your own rhythms, connecting notes, and embellishments.

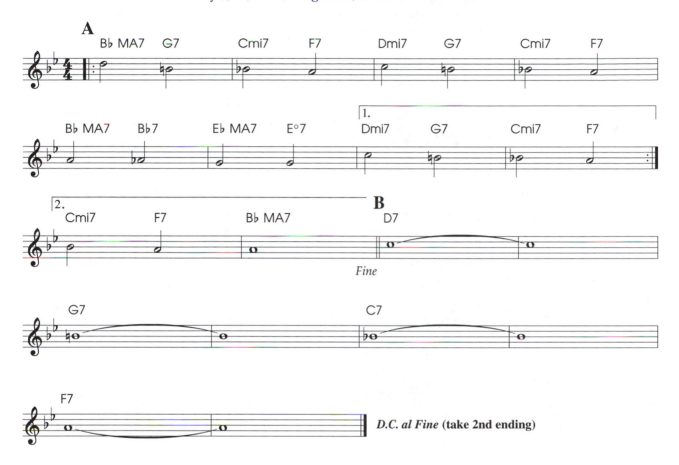

Fine

D.C. al Fine (take 2nd ending)

2. Play the roots, 3rds, and 7ths of each chord, making sure each note has the same duration as the chord. (Note: Diminished chords have minor 3rds and diminished or doubly flatted 7ths.)

3. Although it will not bring out the sound of each individual chord, a single major scale may be used over the chords in the A section. (When improvising, you may wish to lower the A to A♭ in bars 5 and 6.) Use mixolydian scales over the chords in the B section.

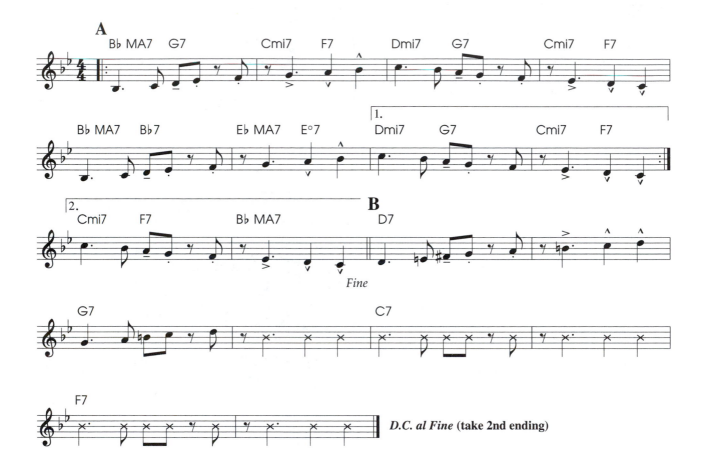

4. The blues scale may also be used over the chords in the A section. Bebop 7th scales are used in the B section.

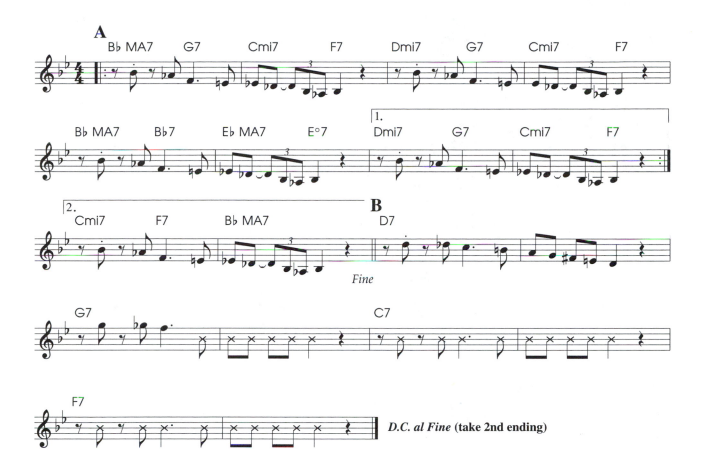

Lester Lept Out

B♭ Instruments
Swing

Scott Reeves

Solos on the form (AABA); use the chord symbols above the melody for your improvisation.

Fine

B♭ Instruments—Exercises for "Lester Lept Out"

1. A guide-tone line that brings out the sound of each chord. After practicing and memorizing the line, improvise a solo based on these pitches, using your own rhythms, connecting notes, and embellishments.

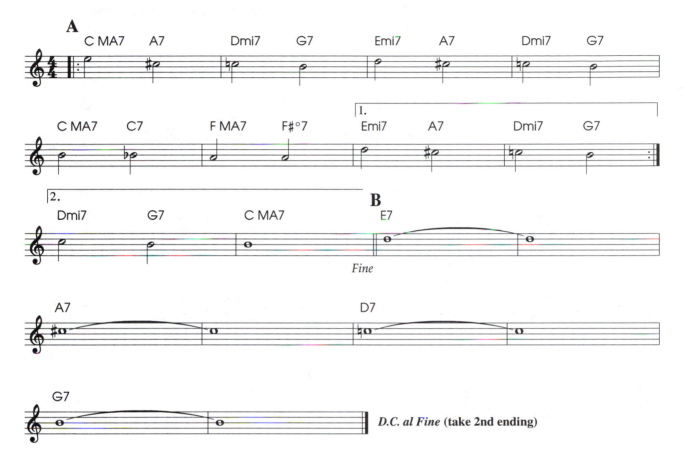

2. Play the roots, 3rds, and 7ths of each chord, making sure each note has the same duration as the chord. (Note: Diminished chords have minor 3rds and diminished or doubly flatted 7ths.)

3. Although it will not bring out the sound of each individual chord, a single major scale may be used over the chords in the A section. (When improvising, you may wish to lower the B to B♭ in bars 5 and 6.) Use mixolydian scales over the chords in the B section.

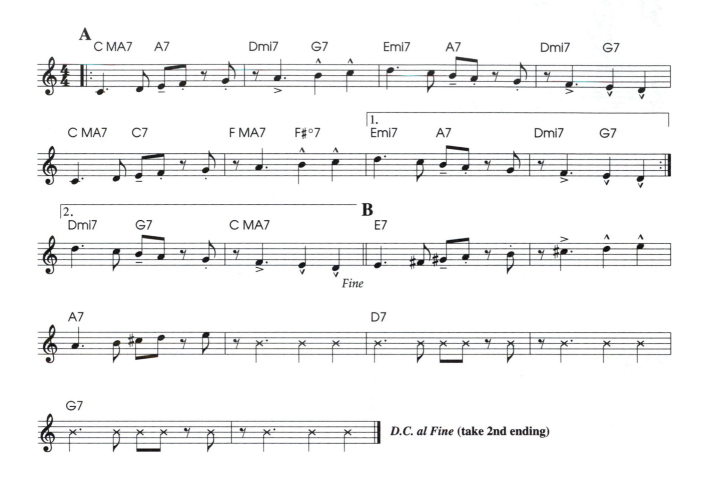

4. The blues scale may also be used over the chords in the A section. Bebop 7th scales are used in the B section.

D.C. al Fine (take 2nd ending)

Lester Lept Out

Eb Instruments
Swing

Scott Reeves

**Solos on the form (AABA); use the chord symbols
above the melody for your improvisation.**

Fine

E♭ Instruments—Exercises for "Lester Lept Out"

1. A guide-tone line that brings out the sound of each chord. After practicing and memorizing the line, improvise a solo based on these pitches, using your own rhythms, connecting notes, and embellishments.

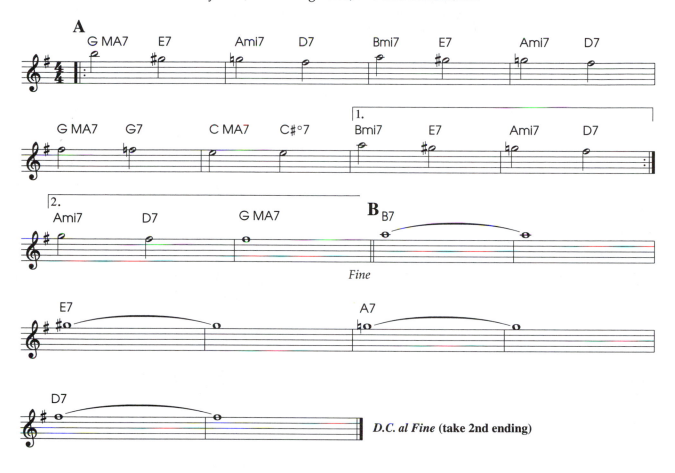

2. Play the roots, 3rds, and 7ths of each chord, making sure each note has the same duration as the chord. (Note: Diminished chords have minor 3rds and diminished or doubly flatted 7ths.)

3. Although it will not bring out the sound of each individual chord, a single major scale may be used over the chords in the A section. (When improvising, you may wish to lower the F♯ to F in bars 5 and 6.) Use mixolydian scales over the chords in the B section.

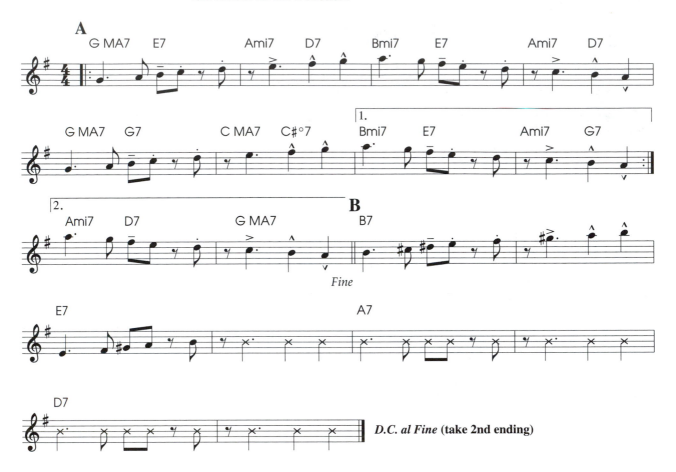

D.C. al Fine (take 2nd ending)

4. The blues scale may also be used over the chords in the A section. Bebop 7th scales are used in the B section.

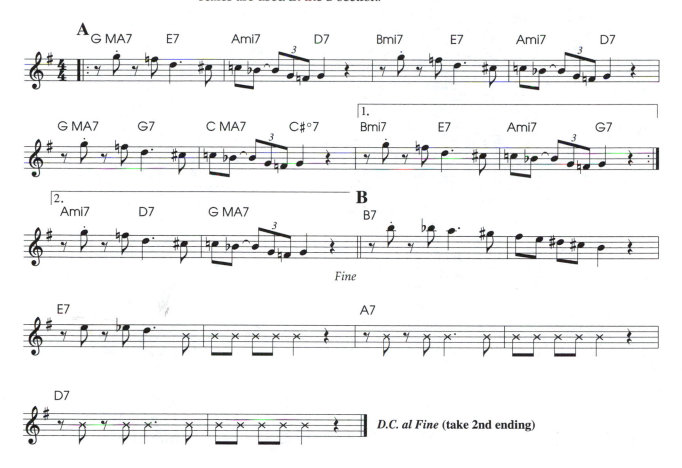

Fine

D.C. al Fine (take 2nd ending)

Lester Lept Out

Bass Clef Instruments
Swing

Scott Reeves

Fine

**Solos on the form (AABA); use the chord symbols
above the melody for your improvisation.**

Bass Clef Instruments—Exercises for "Lester Lept Out"

1. A guide-tone line that brings out the sound of each chord. After practicing and memorizing the line, improvise a solo based on these pitches, using your own rhythms, connecting notes, and embellishments.

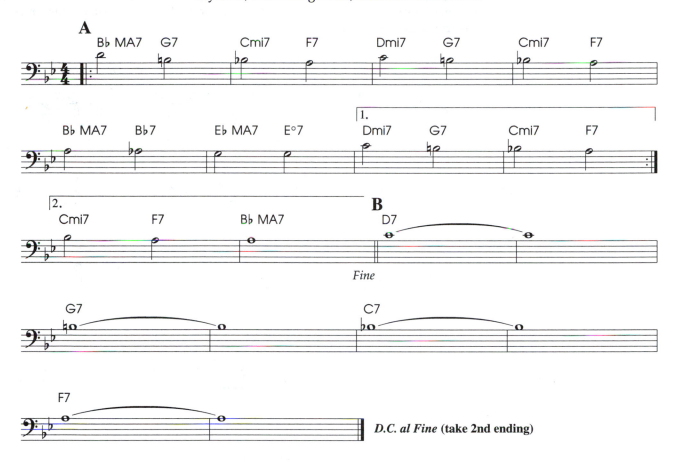

Fine

D.C. al Fine (take 2nd ending)

2. Play the roots, 3rds, and 7ths of each chord, making sure each note has the same duration as the chord. (Note: Diminished chords have minor 3rds and diminished or doubly flatted 7ths.)

3. Although it will not bring out the sound of each individual chord, a single major scale may be used over the chords in the A section. (When improvising, you may wish to lower the A to A♭ in bars 5 and 6.) Use mixolydian scales over the chords in the B section.

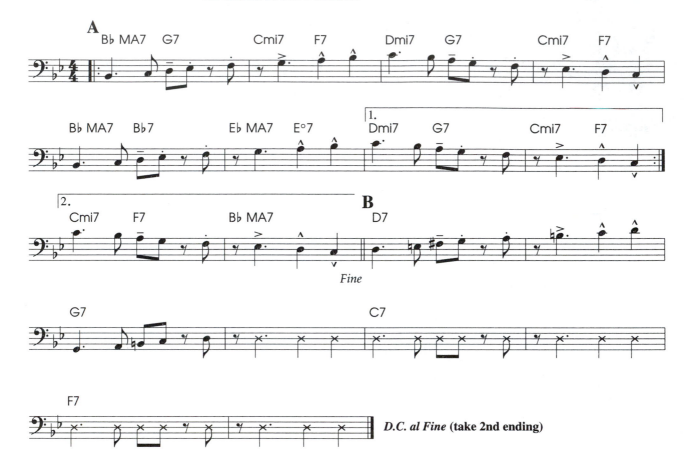

4. The blues scale may also be used over the chords in the A section. Bebop 7th scales are used in the B section.

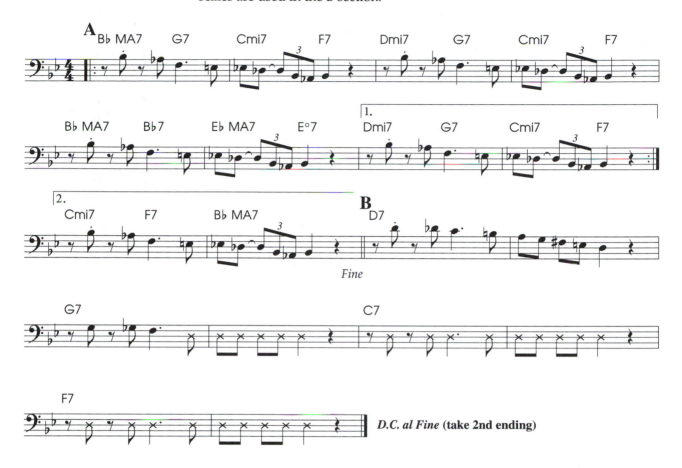

Lester Lept Out

Repeat for solos. After solos,
D.C. al CODA

Lester Lept Out

Bass
Swing

Scott Reeves

Repeat for solos. After solos,
D.C. al CODA

Jazz is not about flashy licks. It's a story with a beginning, middle and end. You must first learn the vocabulary—scales, chords, etc. . . . then let it fly. And be sure to listen inside the rhythm section—that's the motor.

—tenor saxophonist Stan Getz

CHAPTER 10

THE I CHORD IN MINOR; MELODIC, HARMONIC, AND NATURAL MINOR SCALES

In major keys, the minor chord occurs as a ii chord in a ii–V–I progression or as a vi chord in a I–vi–ii–V–I progression. When improvising over a minor ii chord or a minor chord in a modal tune, the dorian scale is usually the preferred choice.[1]

The dorian scale is not the only minor scale used by jazz musicians, however. In minor keys, minor chords function as i (or tonic) chords and as iv (or subdominant) chords. When improvising over tonic minor chords, jazz musicians generally use one of three other types of minor scales: the *natural* (or *aeolian*) *minor,* the *harmonic minor,* and the *melodic minor.* Notice that although all four scales share the same first five notes, they differ in their 6ths and 7ths.

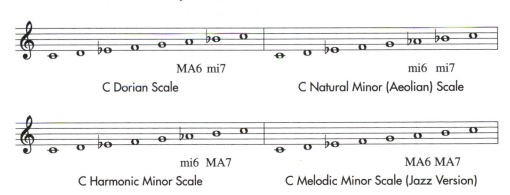

MA6 mi7
C Dorian Scale

mi6 mi7
C Natural Minor (Aeolian) Scale

mi6 MA7
C Harmonic Minor Scale

MA6 MA7
C Melodic Minor Scale (Jazz Version)

[1]Refer to Chapters 6 and 7 to review minor 7th chords and ii–V–I progressions.

The *aeolian* or *natural minor scale* contains the same notes as the major scale a major 6th below.[2]

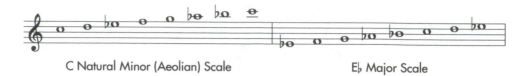

C Natural Minor (Aeolian) Scale   E♭ Major Scale

Major and minor scales related in this way are referred to as the *relative major* and the *relative minor* of each other. Because the scales contain the same notes, a song in a minor key uses the same key signature as its relative major.

Key Signature for C Minor   Key Signature for E♭ Major

The natural minor scale has a sad or dark character. Unlike the dorian scale, which has a tendency to progress to a mixolydian or a major scale, the natural minor scale creates a strong feeling of arrival in a minor key. This is due to its lowered sixth scale degree, which tends to resolve downward a half step to the fifth scale degree, or dominant. The natural minor scale is used over minor 7th chords functioning as i chords in a minor key.

The *harmonic minor scale* can be thought of as a major scale with the third and the sixth notes lowered a half step. This scale has a "Mideastern" or "Asian" quality because of the augmented 2nd between the minor 6th and the major 7th scale degrees.

The *ascending melodic minor scale* can be thought of as a major scale with the third scale degree lowered. (Traditionally, in the descending form of the scale, the sixth and the seventh scale degrees are also lowered, but jazz musicians tend to use only the ascending version of the scale.)

C Harmonic Minor Scale   C Melodic Minor Scale   C Major Scale

Harmonic and melodic minor scales are used when improvising over *minor/major 7th chords,* which consist of a minor triad with a major 7th.

The minor/major 7th chord is fairly *dissonant,* possessing a certain amount of tension. It functions primarily as a i chord in a minor key.

In addition to its use over a minor/major 7th chord, the melodic minor scale colors a minor triad with an added major 6th and a major 9th. This chord is called a *minor 6/9 chord,* although the 6th and the 9th are always major.

[2]Refer to Chapter 14 for more information on intervals.

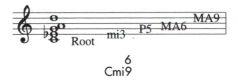

Cmi9

Like the minor/major 7th chord, this chord functions as a tonic minor, but it has a little less "bite" or dissonance. The 6th and the 9th add color and warmth to the sound.

Listen to some jazz standards that contain tonic minor chords, such as "Airegin," "All or Nothing at All," "Alone Together," "Angel Eyes," "Daahoud," "In a Sentimental Mood," "It Don't Mean a Thing," "My Funny Valentine," "Nardis," "Nica's Dream," "Round Midnight," "Solar," "Yesterdays," and "You Don't Know What Love Is." Also practice singing and playing the four types of minor scales to become familiar with their subtle differences in sound and mood.[3]

MELODIC MINOR SCALE WARM-UPS

Play the following exercises over the chord progression, using either a metronome, a live rhythm section, or the "Melodic Minor Warm-Ups" play-along track on the companion CD. Play the written example over the first chord; then use your ear to play the exercise in the different keys indicated by the chord symbols. You will find it helpful to look at the chord progression instead of the exercises when playing in the remaining eleven keys. Pick a tempo at which you can effortlessly play each exercise, gradually moving on to more difficult exercises after you have mastered the easier ones.

Treble Clef C Instruments—Chord Progression

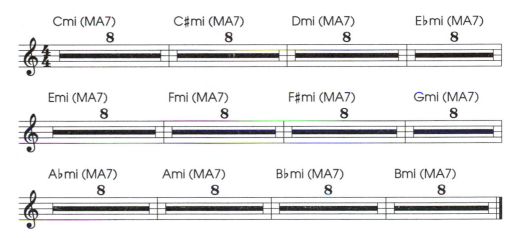

[3]The music to these songs may be found in the following volumes of *A New Approach to Jazz Improvisation:* "Airegin" (Vol. 8), "All or Nothing at All" (Vol. 44), "Alone Together" (Vol. 41), "Angel Eyes" (Vol. 23), "Daahoud" (Vol. 53), "In a Sentimental Mood" (Vol. 12), "It Don't Mean a Thing" (Vol. 59), "My Funny Valentine" (Vol. 25), "Nardis" (Vol. 50), "Nica's Dream" (Vol. 18), "Round Midnight" (Vols. 40 and 56), "Solar" (Vol. 7), "Yesterdays" (Vol. 55), "You Don't Know What Love Is" (Vol. 32).

Treble Clef C Instruments—Beginning Exercises

1. The first five notes of the minor scale:

2. The ascending melodic minor scale:

3. A melodic fragment based on minor scales:

Treble Clef C Instruments—Intermediate Exercises

4. The jazz melodic minor scale, descending:

5. The minor/major 7th arpeggio:

Treble Clef C Instruments—Advanced Exercises

6. A pattern based on the descending minor/major 9th arpeggio:

7. A melodic idea played by trumpeter Freddie Hubbard:

B♭ Instruments—Chord Progression

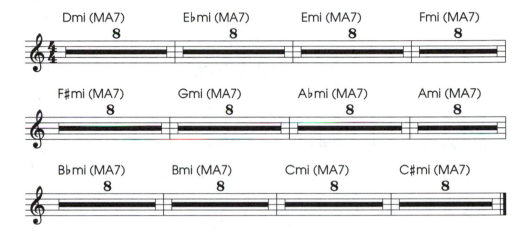

B♭ Instruments—Beginning Exercises

1. The first five notes of the minor scale:

2. The ascending melodic minor scale:

3. A melodic fragment based on minor scales:

B♭ Instruments—Intermediate Exercises

4. The jazz melodic minor scale, descending:

5. The minor/major 7th arpeggio:

B♭ Instruments—Advanced Exercises

6. A pattern based on the descending minor/major 9th arpeggio:

7. A melodic idea played by trumpeter Freddie Hubbard:

E♭ Instruments—Chord Progression

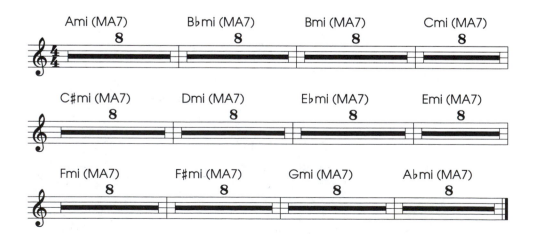

E♭ Instruments—Beginning Exercises

1. The first five notes of the minor scale:

2. The ascending melodic minor scale:

3. A melodic fragment based on minor scales:

E♭ Instruments—Intermediate Exercises

4. The jazz melodic minor scale, descending:

5. The minor/major 7th arpeggio:

E♭ Instruments—Advanced Exercises

6. A pattern based on the descending minor/major 9th arpeggio:

7. A melodic idea played by trumpeter Freddie Hubbard:

Bass Clef Instruments—Chord Progression

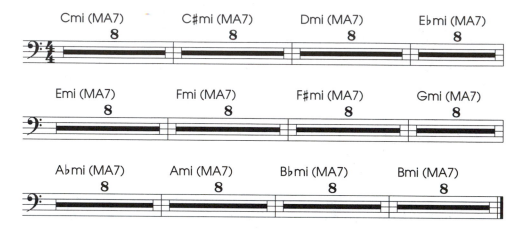

Bass Clef Instruments—Beginning Exercises

1. The first five notes of the minor scale:

2. The ascending melodic minor scale:

3. A melodic fragment based on minor scales:

Bass Clef Instruments—Intermediate Exercises

4. The jazz melodic minor scale, descending:

5. The minor/major 7th arpeggio:

Bass Clef Instruments—Advanced Exercises

6. A pattern based on the descending minor/major 9th arpeggio:

7. A melodic idea played by trumpeter Freddie Hubbard:

All Instruments—Improvisation Exercises

1. Improvise on minor/major 7th chords in all keys, using a live rhythm section or the "Melodic Minor Scale Warm-Ups" play-along track on the companion CD.

2. Make up your own exercises and melodic ideas based on melodic minor scales and minor/major 7th chords.

Improvising on Minor/Major 7th Chords

"Double-Entendre" is a composition in which tonic minor chords are used frequently. Practice and improvise on the song, using either a metronome, a live rhythm section, or the "Double-Entendre" play-along track on the companion CD. (On the CD, the chord progression is played six times.)

    "Double-Entendre" is based on the chord progression to the Duke Ellington composition "It Don't Mean a Thing."[4] The first two measures of the song contain four types of tonic minor chords: a minor triad, a minor/major 7th chord, a minor 7th chord, and a minor 6th chord. The melodic minor scale, in its ascending and descending forms, can be used over all four tonic minor chords. The following is an overview of the chords and their corresponding scales in concert pitch. (Dominant 7th♭9 chords are usually colored by the superlocrian scale, which will be discussed in the following chapter.)

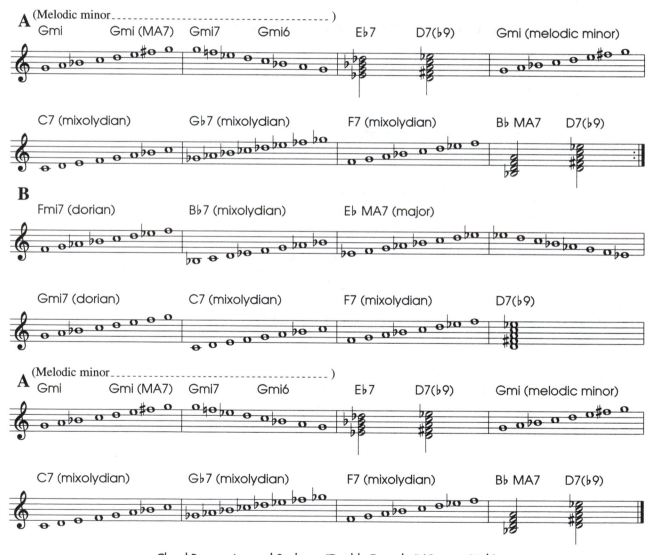

Chord Progression and Scales to "Double-Entendre" (Concert Pitch)

[4]Duke Ellington and Irvings Mills, "It Don't Mean a Thing," copyright 1932, renewed 1960 by Mills Music, Inc., c/o EMI Music Publishing.

Although there are a variety of chords in this tune, most of them are related to one of four primary key areas.[5] The process of improvisation can be greatly simplified by reducing the chord progression to the following:

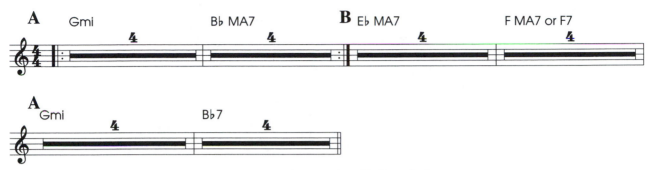

Primary Key Areas in "Double-Entendre"

After playing the melody, practice the chord progression by outlining the chords with the exercises that follow the song.

---

[5]The chords function as diatonic chords, secondary dominants, or tritone substitutions. Refer to Chapter 15 for more information on harmonic analysis.

Double-Entendre

Treble Clef C Instruments

Swing

Scott Reeves

Treble Clef Instruments—Exercises for "Double-Entendre"

1. Play a guide-tone line over the chord progression in which each note lasts the duration of the chord. Start with the 3rd or the 7th of the first chord and move to the 7th or the 3rd of the following chord, whichever is closer.

2. Using the ascending melodic minor scale, 1-2-3-5 patterns, and dorian scales. After playing the exercise as written, try it without looking at the music.

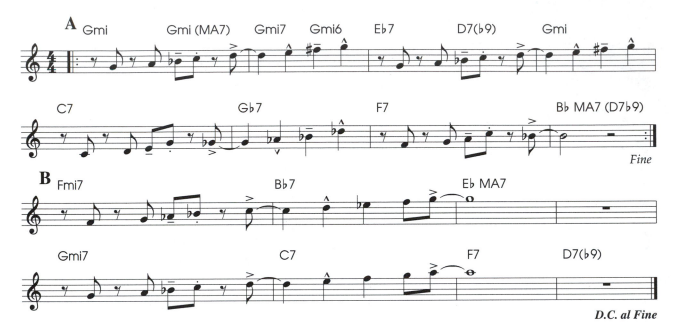

3. Using chord arpeggios. After playing the exercise as written, try it without looking at the music.

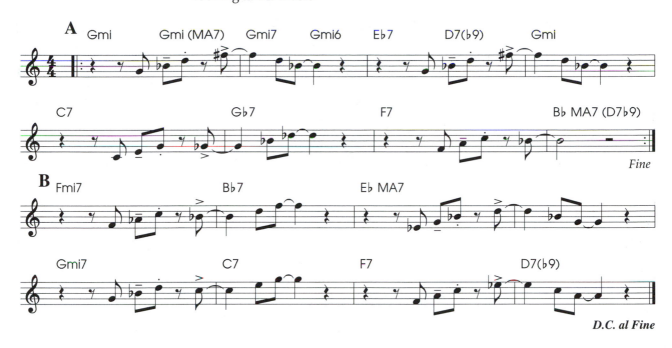

Double-Entendre

B♭ Instruments (tenor sax-play harmony parts *8va*)

Scott Reeves

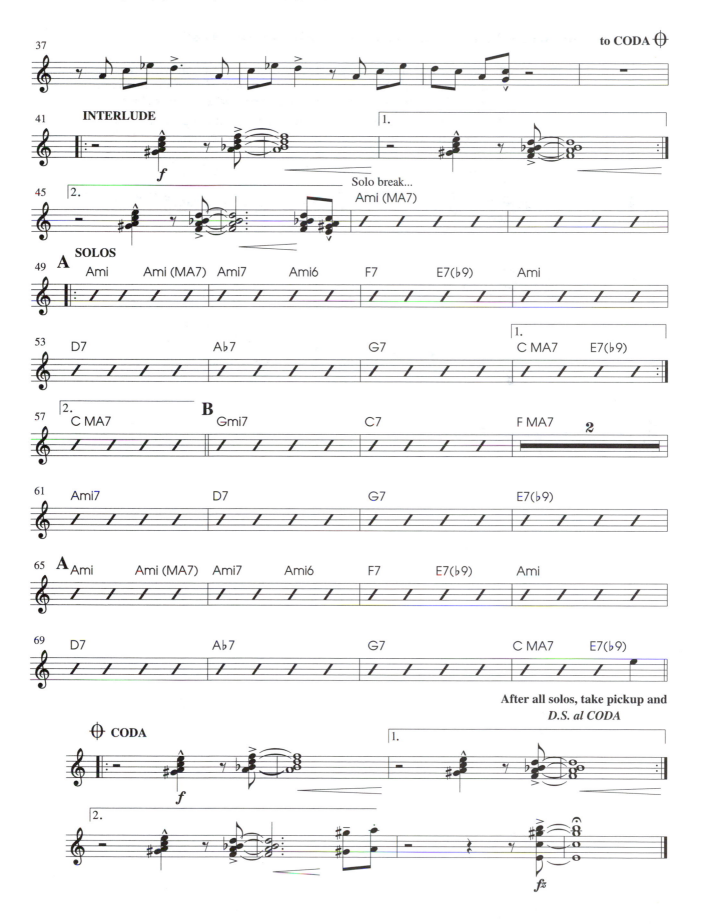

B♭ Instruments—Exercises for "Double-Entendre"

1. Play a guide-tone line over the chord progression in which each note lasts the duration of the chord. Start with the 3rd or the 7th of the first chord and move to the 7th or the 3rd of the following chord, whichever is closer.

2. Using the ascending melodic minor scale, 1-2-3-5 patterns, and dorian scales. After playing the exercise as written, try it without looking at the music.

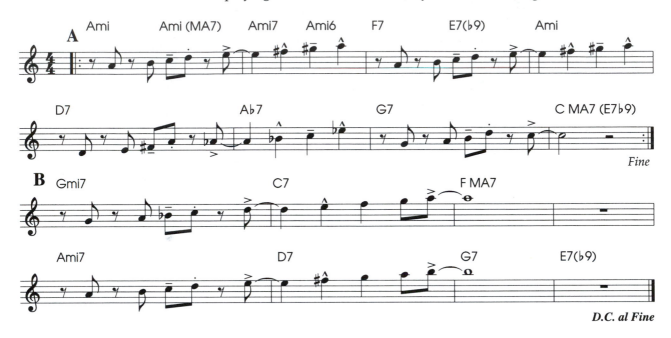

3. Using chord arpeggios. After playing the exercise as written, try it without looking at the music.

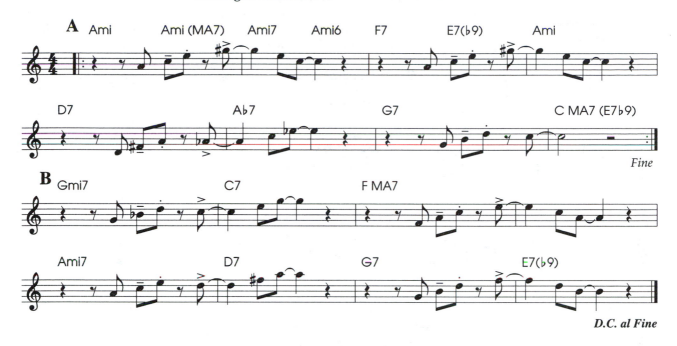

Double-Entendre

Eb **Instruments**

Swing

Scott Reeves

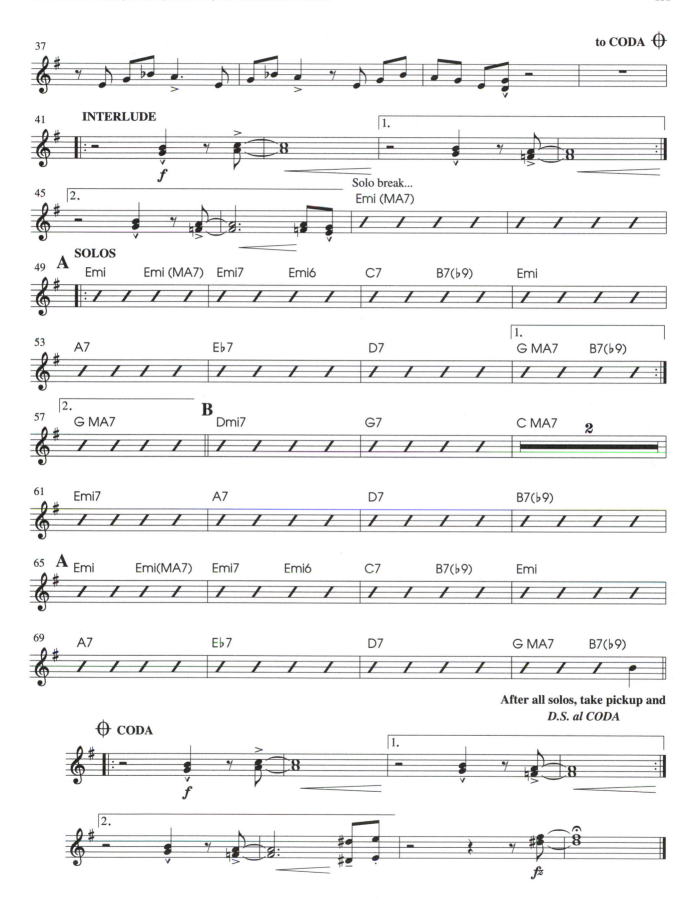

E♭ Instruments—Exercises for "Double-Entendre"

1. Play a guide-tone line over the chord progression in which each note lasts the duration of the chord. Start with the 3rd or the 7th of the first chord and move to the 7th or the 3rd of the following chord, whichever is closer.

2. Using the ascending melodic minor scale, 1-2-3-5 patterns, and dorian scales. After playing the exercise as written, try it without looking at the music.

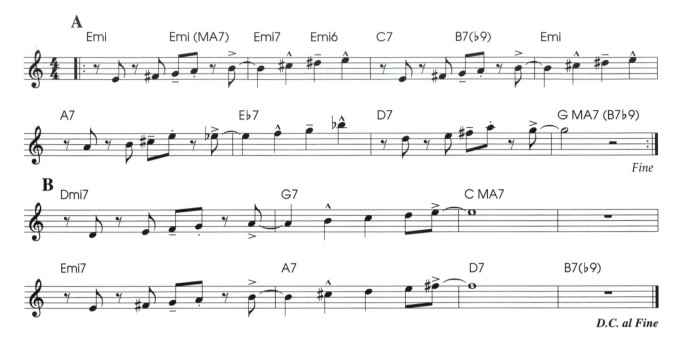

3. Using chord arpeggios. After playing the exercise as written, try it without looking at the music.

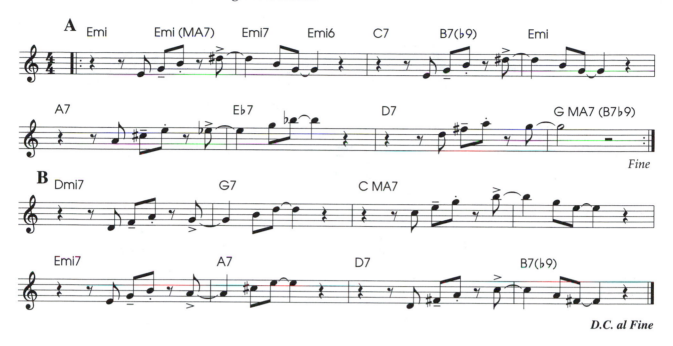

Fine

D.C. al Fine

Double-Entendre

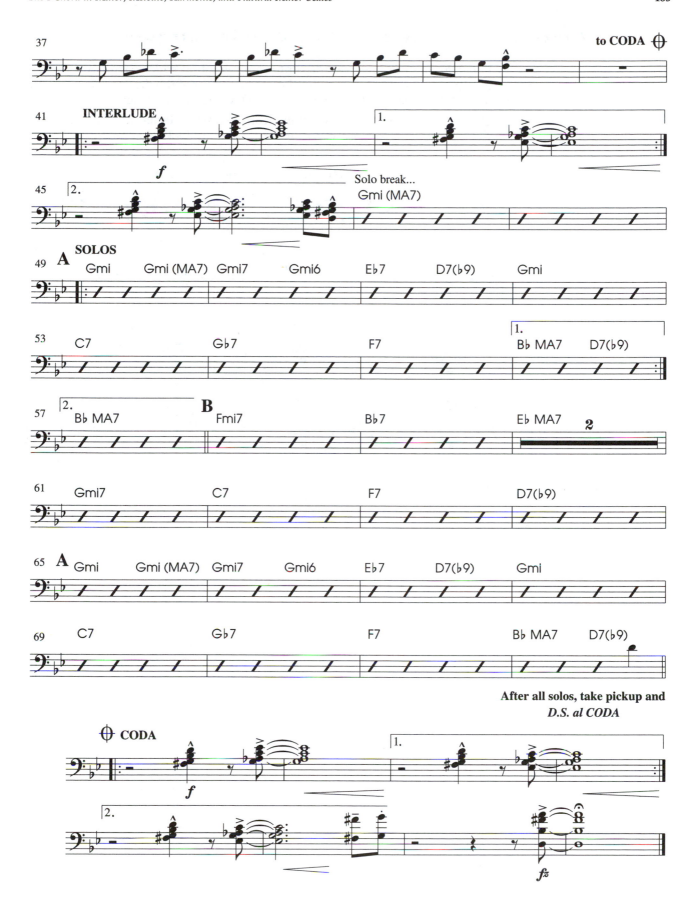

Bass Clef Instruments—Exercises for "Double-Entendre"

1. Play a guide-tone line over the chord progression in which each note lasts the duration of the chord. Start with the 3rd or the 7th of the first chord and move to the 7th or the 3rd of the following chord, whichever is closer.

2. Using the ascending melodic minor scale, 1-2-3-5 patterns, and dorian scales. After playing the exercise as written, try it without looking at the music.

3. Using chord arpeggios. After playing the exercise as written, try it without looking at the music.

Fine

D.C. al Fine

Double-Entendre

For solos, play from the sign 𝄋 (bar 9) to the interlude.
After solos, *D.S. al CODA*

Double-Entendre

Bass
Swing

Scott Reeves

11

THE ii–V–I PROGRESSION IN MINOR; LOCRIAN AND SUPERLOCRIAN SCALES

The ii–V–I progression is the most common chord progression in jazz compositions and standards. In major keys, the ii chord is a minor 7th chord, the V chord is a dominant 7th chord, and the I chord is a major 7th chord.[1] In minor keys, however, the ii chord is a half-diminished 7th chord, the V chord is a dominant 7th chord (often with alterations of the 9th or the 5th or both), and the i chord is a minor chord with either a major 6th, a minor 7th, or a major 7th.

The ii°7–V7♭9–i Progression in C Minor

As we saw in the previous chapter, minor chords functioning as tonic or i chords are colored by one of three tonic minor scales: the natural or aeolian minor, the harmonic minor, and the melodic minor. The natural minor scale is used when improvising over minor 7th chords, the melodic minor scale is used over minor 6th chords, and both the melodic and the harmonic scales can be used over minor/major 7th chords.

A *half-diminished 7th chord* is made up of a root, a minor 3rd, a diminished (or lowered) 5th, and a minor 7th. It can be thought of as a minor 7th chord with the 5th lowered one half step.

---

[1]Refer to Chapter 7 to review the ii–V–I progression in major keys.

D°7 or   Dmi7 Chord
Dmi7♭5 Chord

The half-diminished 7th chord possesses a vague or unresolved quality and has a strong need to progress up a perfect 4th to a dominant chord. It is sometimes extended by the addition of a major 9th or a perfect 11th. The 11th enriches the chord somewhat, and the major 9th adds "bite" or a touch of exoticism to the basic sound.

D°11 (MA9) Chord

For improvising on half-diminished 7th chords, the *locrian scale* is typically used. It contains the same notes as the natural minor scale a whole step below and the major scale a half step above.

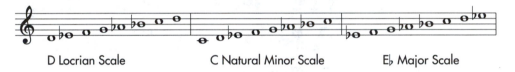

D Locrian Scale   C Natural Minor Scale   E♭ Major Scale

Notice that the locrian scale, played over a ii°7 chord, and the natural minor scale, played over a i7 chord, contain the same notes.

D°7 Chord   D Locrian Scale   Cmi7 Chord   C Natural Minor Scale

The flatted, or *diminished,* fifth scale degree between the first and fifth notes gives the locrian scale a very unstable sound.

Notice that the second note of the locrian scale is lowered a half step. If it were added to the chord, the result would be a minor 9th. Since the minor 9th does not sound good as a member of the half-diminished 7th chord, a major 9th is used instead. The major 9th is derived from an alternative scale choice—the *locrian ♯2 scale,* which is identical to a locrian scale with a raised second scale degree.

D Locrian ♯2 Scale   D Locrian Scale

The V7 chord in minor is referred to as an *altered dominant;* the 9ths of the chord are always altered, and the 5ths are often raised or lowered as well. The dominant 7th ♭9 is very unstable and has a strong tendency to resolve down a perfect 5th to a i chord. The dominant 7th ♯9 chord is more stable and has a "funky" or "bluesy" quality. Often, the ♯9th will move to a ♭9th or vice versa.

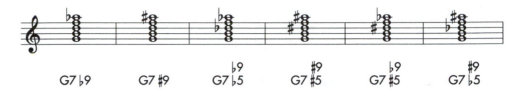

However, altered 9ths never move to major or unaltered 9ths. When altered 5ths are added to altered 9th chords, the amount of tension or dissonance increases. The dominant 7th ♯9 ♯5 is the most common combination.

The scale that fits the V7 chord in minor is known variously as the *super-locrian scale,* the *diminished/whole-tone scale,* and the *altered scale.* It contains all possible alterations of the 9ths and the 5ths.

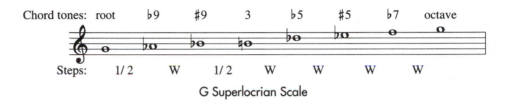

G Superlocrian Scale

The first half of this scale alternates half steps and whole steps, and the second part is made up entirely of whole steps. The superlocrian scale contains the same notes as the melodic minor scale a half step above, giving it the same relationship to melodic minor as locrian has to major.

The diminished/whole-tone scale has a dark, mysterious quality. To familiarize yourself with this scale and with the minor ii–V7–i progression, listen to jazz standards such as "Autumn Leaves," "Blue in Green," "How Insensitive," "Invitation," "My One and Only Love," "Soul Eyes," "The Shadow of Your Smile," and "Yesterdays."[2]

---

iiø7–V7♭9–i WARM-UPS

Play the following exercises over the chord progression, using either a metronome, a live rhythm section, or the "iiø7–V7♭9–i Progression Warm-Ups" play-along track on the companion CD. Play the written example over the first chord; then use your ear to play the exercise in the different keys indicated by the chord symbols. You will find it helpful to look at the chord progression instead of

---

[2]The music to these songs may be found in the following volumes of *A New Approach to Jazz Improvisation:* "Autumn Leaves" (Vol. 44), "Blue in Green" (Vol. 50), "How Insensitive" (Vol. 31), "Invitation" (Vol. 34), "My One and Only Love" (Vol. 51), "Soul Eyes" (Vol. 32), "The Shadow of Your Smile" (Vol. 34), "Yesterdays" (Vol. 55).

the exercises when playing in the remaining eleven keys. Pick a tempo at which you can effortlessly play each exercise, gradually moving on to more difficult exercises after you have mastered the easier ones.

Treble Clef C Instruments—Chord Progression

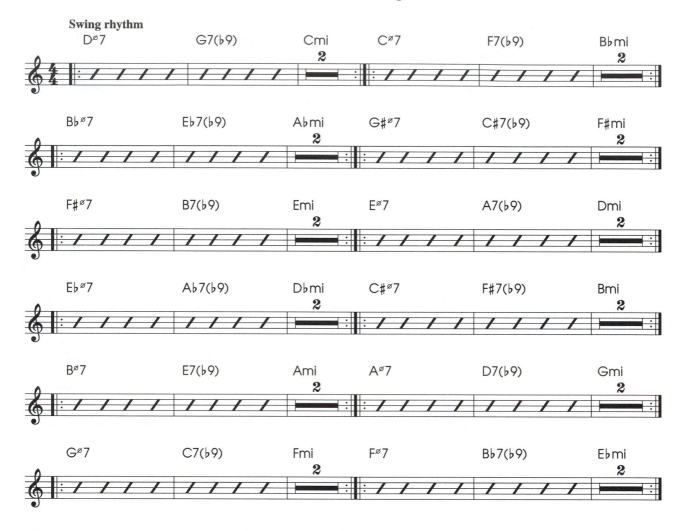

Treble Clef C Instruments—Beginning Exercises

1. Using the locrian scale over the entire progression:

2. Using the first four notes of the superlocrian scale over the entire progression:

Treble Clef C Instruments—Intermediate Exercises

3. The ascending locrian scale:

4. The ascending superlocrian scale:

5. Half-diminished 7th and dominant 7th ♭9 arpeggios:

Treble Clef C Instruments—Advanced Exercises

6. A descending pattern that uses both the locrian and the superlocrian scales:

7. A pattern that outlines the ♯9th, the ♭9th, and the ♯5th of the V7 chord:

B♭ Instruments—Chord Progression

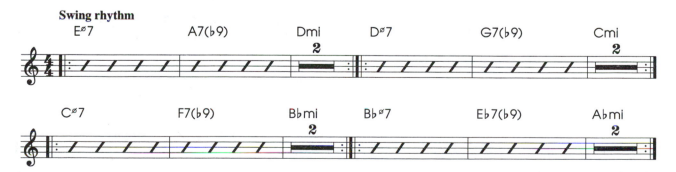

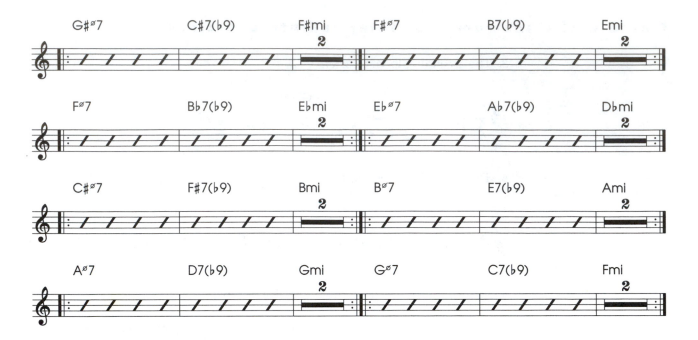

B♭ Instruments—Beginning Exercises

1. Using the locrian scale over the entire progression:

2. Using the first four notes of the superlocrian scale over the entire progression:

B♭ Instruments—Intermediate Exercises

3. The ascending locrian scale:

4. The ascending superlocrian scale:

5. Half-diminished 7th and dominant 7th ♭9 arpeggios:

B♭ Instruments—Advanced Exercises

6. A descending pattern that uses both the locrian and the superlocrian scales:

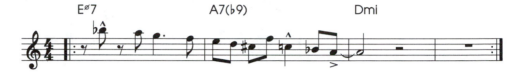

7. A pattern that outlines the ♯9th, the ♭9th, and the ♯5th of the V7 chord:

E♭ Instruments—Chord Progression

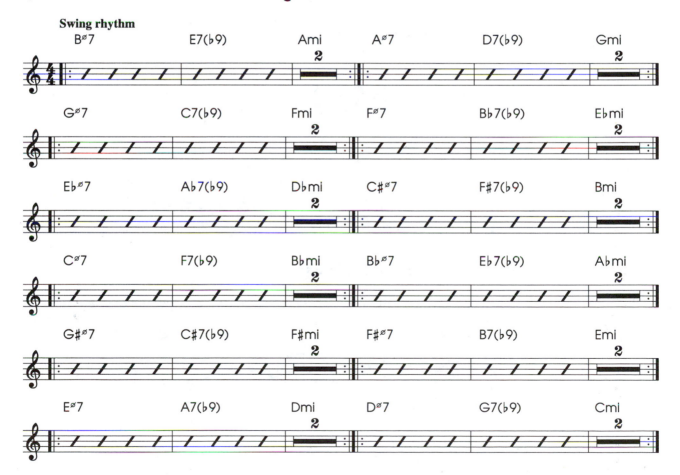

E♭ Instruments—Beginning Exercises

1. Using the locrian scale over the entire progression:

2. Using the first four notes of the superlocrian scale over the entire progression:

E♭ Instruments—Intermediate Exercises

3. The ascending locrian scale:

4. The ascending superlocrian scale:

5. Half-diminished 7th and dominant 7th ♭9 arpeggios:

E♭ Instruments—Advanced Exercises

6. A descending pattern that uses both the locrian and the superlocrian scales:

7. A pattern that outlines the ♯9th, the ♭9th, and the ♯5th of the V7 chord:

Bass Clef Instruments—Chord Progression

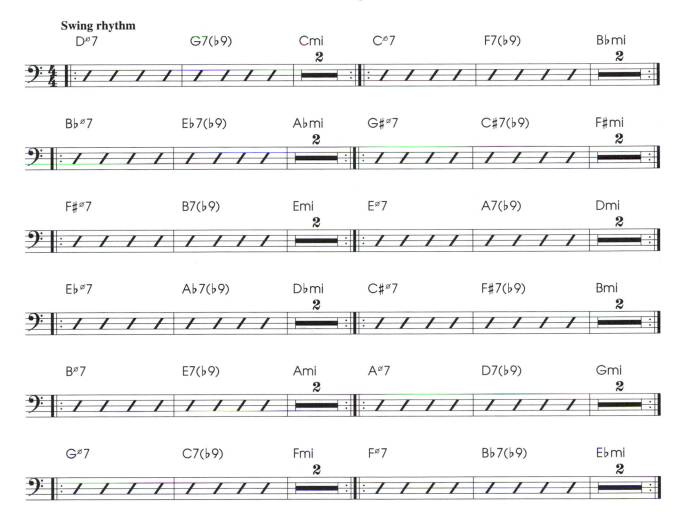

Bass Clef Instruments—Beginning Exercises

1. Using the locrian scale over the entire progression:

2. Using the first four notes of the superlocrian scale over the entire progression:

Bass Clef Instruments—Intermediate Exercises

3. The ascending locrian scale:

4. The ascending superlocrian scale:

5. Half-diminished 7th and dominant 7th ♭9 arpeggios:

Bass Clef Instruments—Advanced Exercises

6. A descending pattern that uses both the locrian and the superlocrian scales:

7. A pattern that outlines the ♯9th, the ♭9th, and the ♯5th of the V7 chord:

All Instruments—Improvisation Exercises

1. Improvise on minor ii⌀7–V7–i progressions in all keys, using a live rhythm section or the "ii⌀7–V7♭9–i Progression Warm-Ups" play-along track on the companion CD.

2. Make up your own exercises and melodic ideas based on locrian and super-locrian scales and minor ii⌀7–V7–i progressions.

♩MPROVISING ii⌀7–V7–i PROGRESSIONS

"Blue Autumn" is a composition based on the chord progression to the song "Autumn Leaves," and uses ii–V–I progressions in major and minor keys.[3] Practice and improvise on the song, using either a metronome, a live rhythm section, or the "Blue Autumn" play-along track on the companion CD. (On the CD, the chord progression is played six times.)

Since most of the chords in "Blue Autumn" belong to ii–V–I progressions in B♭ major and its relative minor of G minor, there are a great many common tones throughout. The scales in concert pitch are as follows:

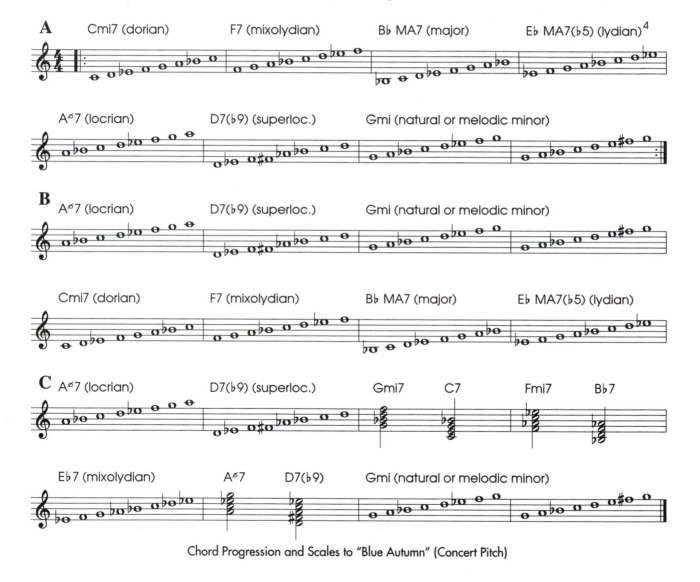

Chord Progression and Scales to "Blue Autumn" (Concert Pitch)

---

[3]Joseph Kosma and Johnny Mercer, "Autumn Leaves," copyright 1947 and 1950, renewed 1975 and 1978 by Enoch et Cie.

[4]Refer to Chapter 15 for further information on lydian scales

Because most of these chords are related, the harmony can be simplified to the following primary key areas:

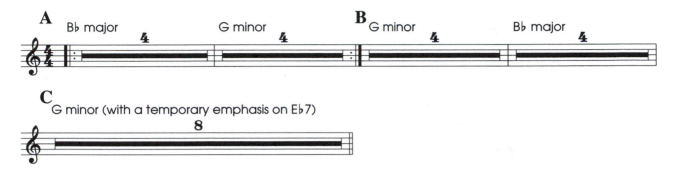

Primary Key Areas in "Blue Autumn"

After playing the melody, practice the chord progression by outlining the chords with the exercises that follow the song.

Blue Autumn

Treble Clef C Instruments

Swing

Scott Reeves

Fine

Solos on the form (AABC). Use the chord symbols above the melody for your improvisation. After solos, *D.S. al Fine*

Treble Clef C Instruments—Exercises for "Blue Autumn"

Practice each exercise for "Blue Autumn" as follows:

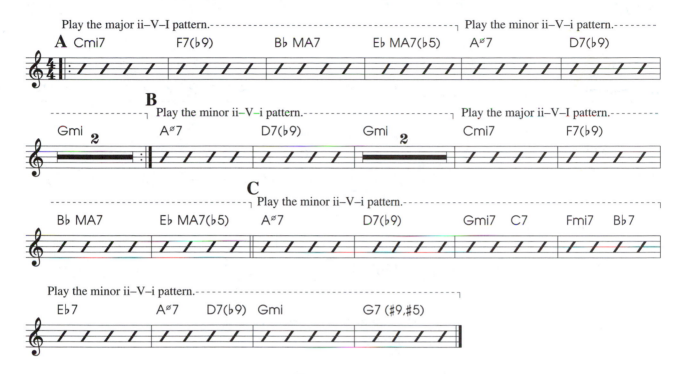

Play the major ii–V–I pattern. - Play the minor ii–V–i pattern. - - - - - - - -

A Cmi7   F7(b9)   Bb MA7   Eb MA7(b5)   A∅7   D7(b9)

- - - - - - - - - - - - - - - - Play the minor ii–V–i pattern. - Play the major ii–V–I pattern. - - - - - - - -

B Gmi 2   A∅7   D7(b9)   Gmi 2   Cmi7   F7(b9)

- Play the minor ii–V–i pattern. -

C Bb MA7   Eb MA7(b5)   A∅7   D7(b9)   Gmi7   C7   Fmi7   Bb7

Play the minor ii–V–i pattern. -

Eb7   A∅7   D7(b9)   Gmi   G7 (#9,#5)

1. Using the dorian and locrian scales over the major and minor ii–V–I's:

    a. Major ii–V–I pattern:

Cmi7   F7   Bb MA7   Eb MA7(b5)

    b. Minor ii–V–i pattern:

A∅7   D7(b9)   Gmi

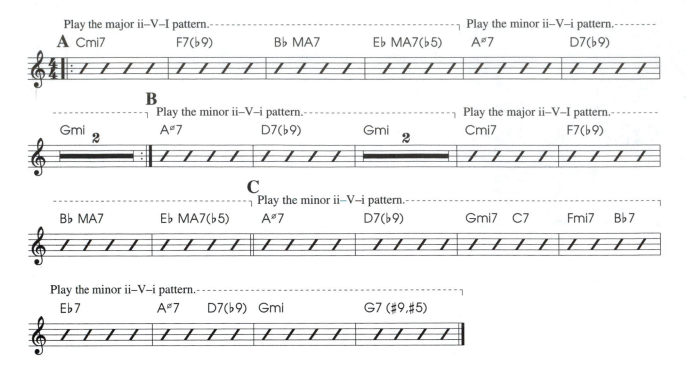

2. Minor 7th, half-diminished 7th, and dominant 7th ♭9 arpeggios:

    a. Major ii–V–I pattern:

    b. Minor ii–V–i pattern:

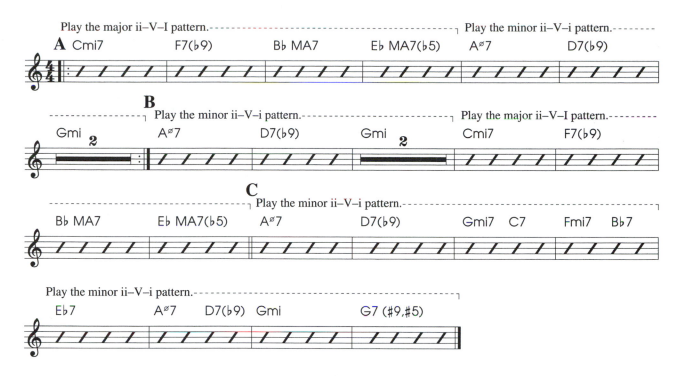

3. A pattern that outlines the #9, the ♭9, and the #5 of the V chord:

   a. Major ii–V–I pattern:

   b. Minor ii–V–i pattern:

Blue Autumn

Solos on the form (AABC). Use the chord symbols above the melody for your improvisation. After solos,
D.S. al Fine

B♭ Instruments—Exercises for "Blue Autumn"

Practice each exercise for "Blue Autumn" as follows:

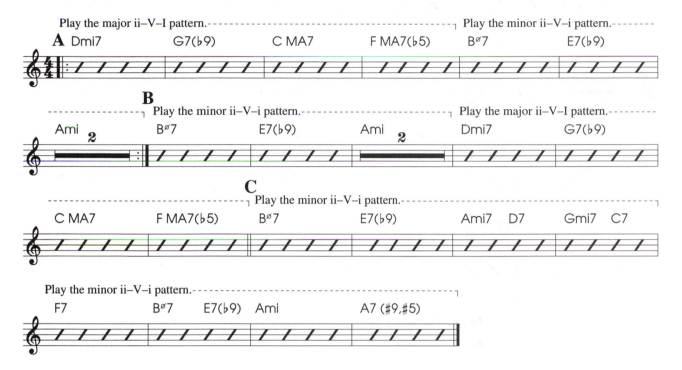

1. Using the dorian and locrian scales over the major and minor ii–V–I's:

   a. Major ii–V–I pattern:

   b. Minor ii–V–i pattern:

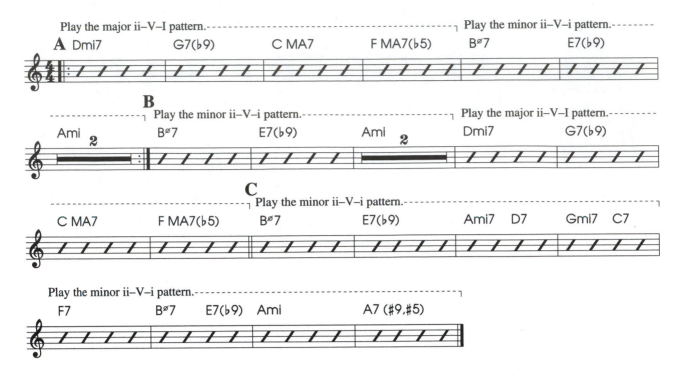

2. Minor 7th, half-diminished 7th, and dominant 7th ♭9 arpeggios:

a. Major ii–V–I pattern:

b. Minor ii–V–i pattern:

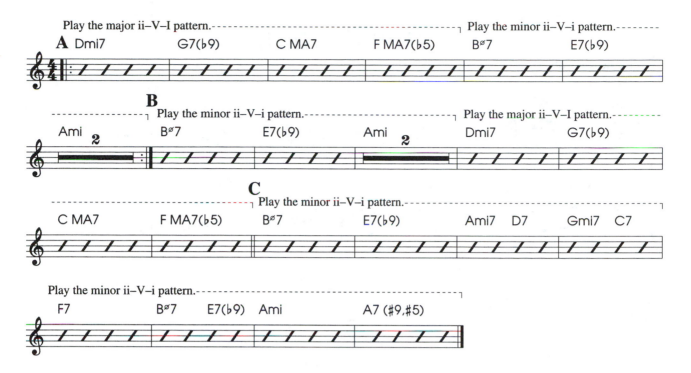

3. A pattern that outlines the ♯9, the ♭9, and the ♯5 of the V chord:

    a. Major ii–V–I pattern:

    b. Minor ii–V–i pattern:

Blue Autumn

Solos on the form (AABC). Use the chord symbols above the melody for your improvisation. After solos, *D.S. al Fine*

E♭ Instruments—Exercises for "Blue Autumn"

Practice each exercise for "Blue Autumn" as follows:

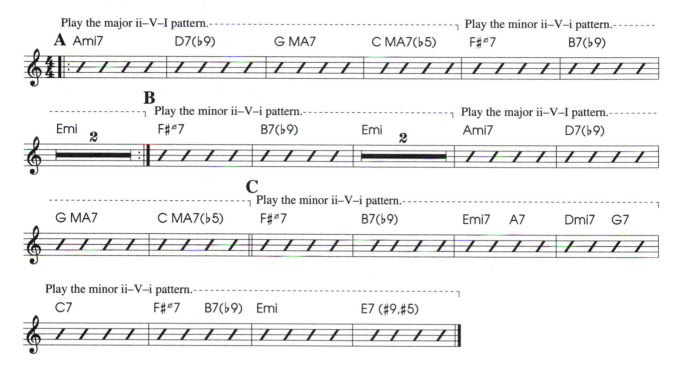

1. Using the dorian and locrian scales over the major and minor ii–V–I's:

a. Major ii–V–I pattern:

b. Minor ii–V–i pattern:

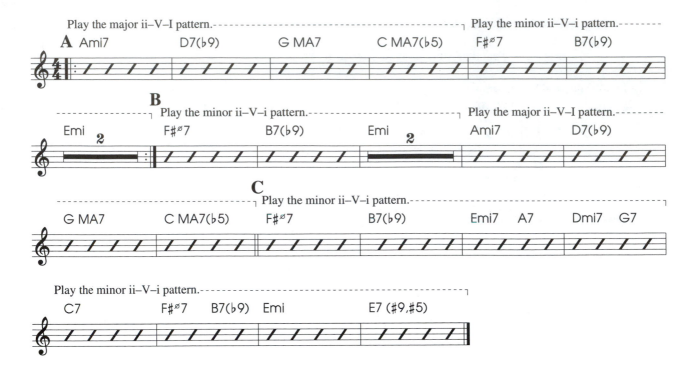

2. Minor 7th, half-diminished 7th, and dominant 7th♭9 arpeggios:

   a. Major ii–V–I pattern:

   b. Minor ii–V–i pattern:

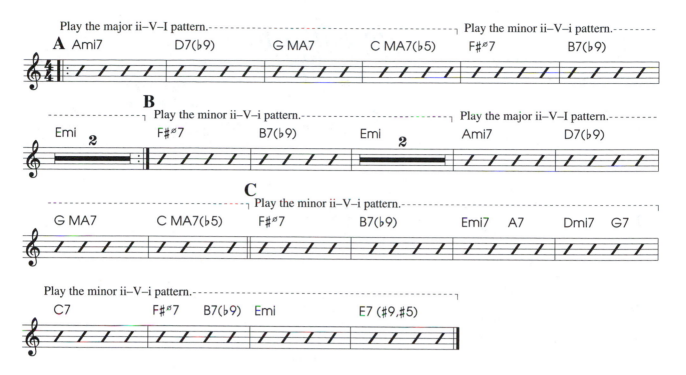

3. A pattern that outlines the ♯9, the ♭9, and the ♯5 of the V chord:

   a. Major ii–V–I pattern:

   b. Minor ii–V–i pattern:

Blue Autumn

Bass Clef Instruments
Swing

Scott Reeves

Solos on the form (AABC). Use the chord symbols above the melody for your improvisation. After solos, ***D.S. al Fine***

Bass Clef Instruments—Exercises for "Blue Autumn"

Practice each exercise for "Blue Autumn" as follows:

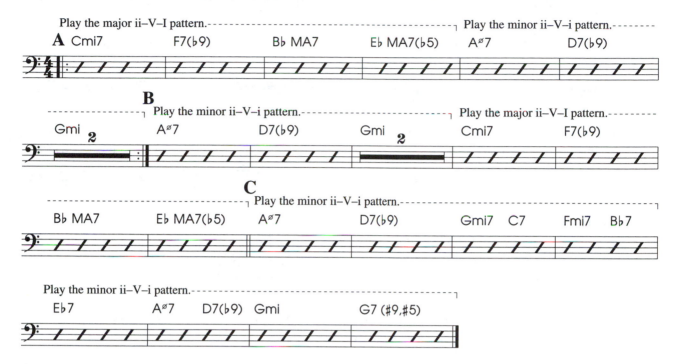

1. Using the dorian and locrian scales over the major and minor ii–V–I's:

   a. Major ii–V–I pattern:

   b. Minor ii–V–i pattern:

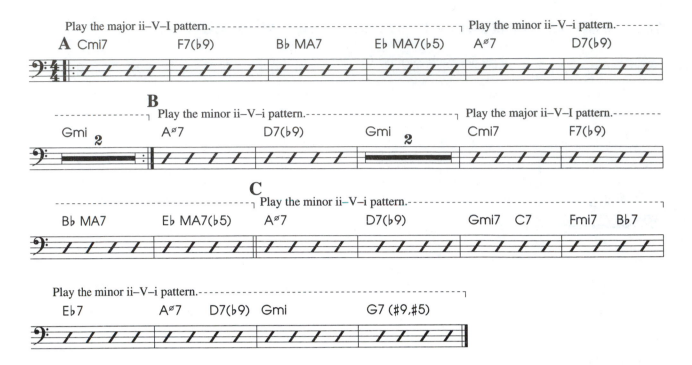

Play the major ii–V–I pattern.-------------------------------- Play the minor ii–V–i pattern.--------

A Cmi7   F7(♭9)   B♭ MA7   E♭ MA7(♭5)   A⌀7   D7(♭9)

-------------- **B** Play the minor ii–V–i pattern.------------------------- Play the major ii–V–I pattern.---------

Gmi **2**   A⌀7   D7(♭9)   Gmi **2**   Cmi7   F7(♭9)

C Play the minor ii–V–i pattern.-------------------------

B♭ MA7   E♭ MA7(♭5)   A⌀7   D7(♭9)   Gmi7   C7   Fmi7   B♭7

Play the minor ii–V–i pattern.------------------------------------

E♭7   A⌀7   D7(♭9)   Gmi   G7 (♯9,♯5)

2. Minor 7th, half-diminished 7th, and dominant 7th ♭9 arpeggios:

a. Major ii–V–I pattern:

Cmi7   F7(♭9)   B♭ MA7   E♭ MA7(♭5)

b. Minor ii–V–i pattern:

A⌀7   D7(♭9)   Gmi

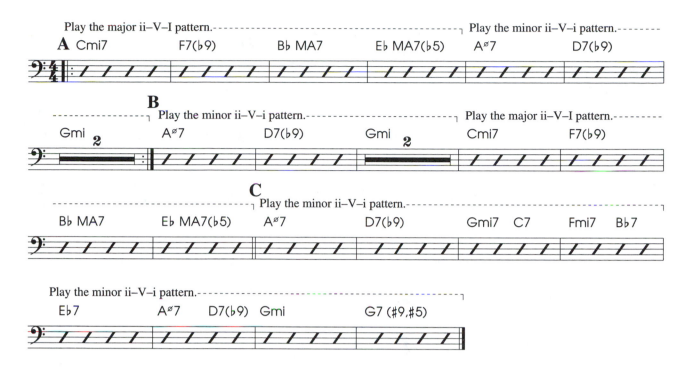

3. A pattern that outlines the ♯9, the ♭9, and the ♯5 of the V chord:

   a. Major ii–V–I pattern:

   b. Minor ii–V–i pattern:

Blue Autumn

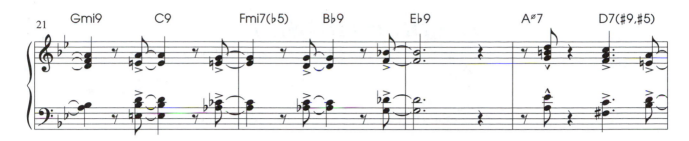

Fine

Solos on the form (AABC). Use the chord symbols above the chords for your improvisation. After solos,
D.S. al Fine

Blue Autumn

Solos on the form (AABC). Use the chord symbols above the bass line for your improvisation. After solos, *D.S. al Fine*

*It's a given that . . . you have to play hip notes,
have to play with a good groove, play deep
inside the changes, play over the changes, play
outside the changes. Some people make careers
out of the fundamentals—but I think (that) to
go to the next level you have to find your own
way of looking at music, thinking about melody,
sound and what music is to you.*

—guitarist Pat Metheny

CHAPTER

12

PENTATONIC SCALES

All pentatonic scales contain five notes, exclusive of the octave. There are numerous types of pentatonic scales, many of which are found in music from Asia and Africa. Although some jazz artists, such as Yusef Lateef and John Coltrane, have explored a variety of pentatonic scales from other cultures, most jazz musicians commonly use *major* and *minor pentatonic scales.*

The *major pentatonic scale* can be thought of as a major scale with the fourth and seventh notes omitted.

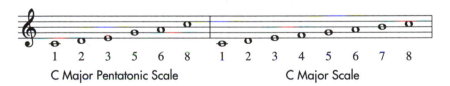

| 1 | 2 | 3 | 5 | 6 | 8 | 1 | 2 | 3 | 4 | 5 | 6 | 7 | 8 |

C Major Pentatonic Scale   C Major Scale

The major pentatonic has a "pretty" or happy quality and a sound reminiscent of certain Japanese melodies. Like the major scale, it can be used when improvising over major 7th chords and, because it lacks a 7th, over dominant 7th chords as well.

C MA7   C7   C Major Pentatonic Scale

Because of the two "missing" notes, major pentatonic scales built on the 5th and the 9th of the chord may also be used when improvising over major 7th chords. Each of these three scales emphasizes different chord tones.

The *minor pentatonic scale* can be thought of as a natural (aeolian) minor scale with the second and the sixth notes omitted or as a blues scale with the lowered fifth note omitted.

The minor pentatonic scale has a mournful character and can be used when improvising over minor 7th and dominant 7th ♯9 chords.

Minor pentatonic scales built on the 5th and the 9th of the chord may also be used when improvising on minor 7th chords.

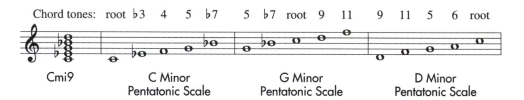

The *minor/added 6th pentatonic scale* is a variation of the minor pentatonic scale. It replaces the minor 7th with the major 6th. John Coltrane used it extensively in his improvisations on compositions such as "Your Lady," "Impressions," and "Softly as in a Morning Sunrise."[1]

C Minor/Added 6th Pentatonic Scale

[1]Scott D. Reeves, *Creative Jazz Improvisation,* 2nd ed. (Englewood Cliffs, N.J.: Prentice Hall, 1995), p. 218.

In addition to their use over certain chords, major and minor pentatonic scales are used to intentionally "violate" or "go outside" the normal chords. The improvisor typically does this by playing the "correct," or "inside," scale choices at the beginning of the phrase, departing from the key in the middle, and returning to the tonal center at the end of the phrase. When done by masters such as John Coltrane, McCoy Tyner, and Woody Shaw, playing "outside" the changes can create exciting dissonances and resolutions; when musicians less competent at chordal improvisation attempt the technique, they can sound as if they are lost or unfamiliar with the chords.

Pentatonic scales may be used when improvising on any songs that contain major 7th, minor 7th, or dominant 7th chords. However, certain compositions, such as "A Love Supreme," "Blues Minor," "Bolivia," "Cantiloupe Island," "Dear Lord," "Footprints," "Impressions," "Little Sunflower," "Maiden Voyage," "Milestones" (new version), "St. Thomas," "So What," "Spiritual," "The Promise," and "Yes or No," are particularly well suited for the use of pentatonic scales.[2]

MINOR PENTATONIC SCALE WARM-UPS

Play the following exercises over the chord progression, using either a metronome, a live rhythm section, or the "Minor Pentatonic Warm-Ups" play-along track on the companion CD. Play the written example over the first chord; then use your ear to play the exercise in the different keys indicated by the chord symbols. You will find it helpful to look at the chord progression instead of the exercises when playing in the remaining eleven keys. Pick a tempo at which you can effortlessly play each exercise, gradually moving on to more difficult exercises after you have mastered the easier ones.

Treble Clef C Instruments—Chord Progression

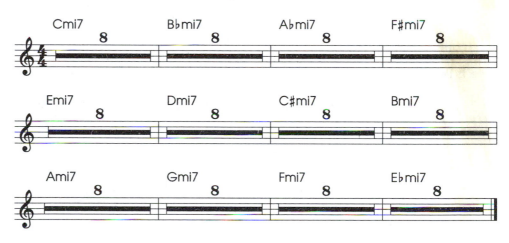

[2]The music to these songs may be found in the following volumes of *A New Approach to Jazz Improvisation:* "A Love Supreme" (Vol. 28), "Dear Lord" (Vol. 28), "Blues Minor" (Vol. 27), "Bolivia" (Vol. 35), "Cantiloupe Island" (Vols. 11 and 54), "Footprints" (Vols. 33 and 54), "Impressions" (Vols. 28 and 54), "Little Sunflower" (Vol. 60), "Maiden Voyage" (Vols. 11 and 54), "Milestones" (new version) (Vol. 50), "The Promise" (Vol. 27), "St. Thomas" (Vol. 8), "So What" (Vol. 50), "Spiritual" (Vol. 27), "Yes or No" (Vol. 33).

Treble Clef C Instruments—Beginning Exercises

1. The first four notes of the minor pentatonic scale:

2. The entire minor pentatonic scale:

Treble Clef C Instruments—Intermediate Exercises

3. The minor pentatonic scale built on the 5th of the chord:

4. A descending minor pentatonic pattern:

Treble Clef C Instruments—Advanced Exercises

5. A descending pattern based on 4ths and arpeggios:

6. A stepwise descending pattern:

B♭ Instruments—Chord Progression

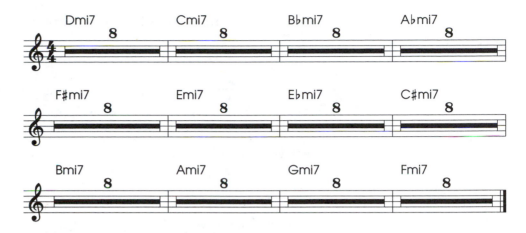

B♭ Instruments—Beginning Exercises

1. The first four notes of the minor pentatonic scale:

2. The entire minor pentatonic scale:

B♭ Instruments—Intermediate Exercises

3. The minor pentatonic scale built on the 5th of the chord:

4. A descending minor pentatonic pattern:

B♭ Instruments—Advanced Exercises

5. A descending pattern based on 4ths and arpeggios:

6. A stepwise descending pattern:

E♭ Instruments—Chord Progression

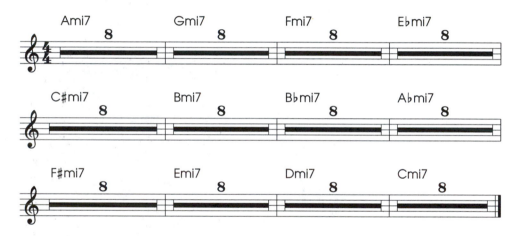

E♭ Instruments—Beginning Exercises

1. The first four notes of the minor pentatonic scale:

2. The entire minor pentatonic scale:

E♭ Instruments—Intermediate Exercises

3. The minor pentatonic scale built on the 5th of the chord:

4. A descending minor pentatonic pattern:

E♭ Instruments—Advanced Exercises

5. A descending pattern based on 4ths and arpeggios:

6. A stepwise descending pattern:

Bass Clef Instruments—Chord Progression

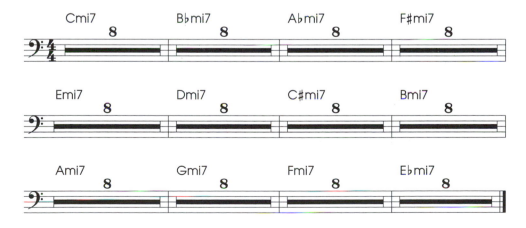

Bass Clef Instruments—Beginning Exercises

1. The first four notes of the minor pentatonic scale:

2. The entire minor pentatonic scale:

Bass Clef Instruments—Intermediate Exercises

3. The minor pentatonic scale built on the 5th of the chord:

4. A descending minor pentatonic pattern:

Bass Clef Instruments—Advanced Exercises

5. A descending pattern based on 4ths and arpeggios:

6. A stepwise descending pattern:

All Instruments—Improvisation Exercises

1. Improvise on major and minor pentatonic scales in all keys, using a live rhythm section or any of the play-along tracks to Chapters 4, 5, 6, 8, and 13.

2. Make up your own exercises and melodic ideas based on major and minor pentatonic scales.

♩MPROVISING ON MINOR PENTATONIC SCALES

"El Corazón" is a minor blues with a 6/4 Latin rhythm. Practice and improvise on the song, using either a metronome, a live rhythm section, or the "El Corazón" play-along track on the companion CD. (On the CD, the chord progression is played ten times.)

Like most blues, "El Corazón" is based on a 12-bar form consisting of three 4-bar phrases. Unlike the chords in "Eta Carina Blue," the i and iv chords are minor, the ii chord is half-diminished, and the V chord is altered.[3] The 6/4 Latin rhythm adds to the pensive mood of the song and encourages the improvisor to employ space, 2-against-3 polyrhythms, and melodic phrasing when soloing. (Remember that eighth notes in a Latin rhythm should be played fairly evenly.)

The harmonic aspect of the song can be addressed by using a single minor pentatonic or blues scale over all the chords or by drawing on the scales that fit each chord in the progression.

1. Using the D minor pentatonic or D blues scale over the entire progression:

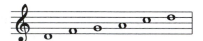   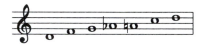

---

[3]Refer to Chapter 8 for more information on the blues form and "Eta Carina Blue."

2. Using dorian, locrian, and superlocrian scales over each chord:

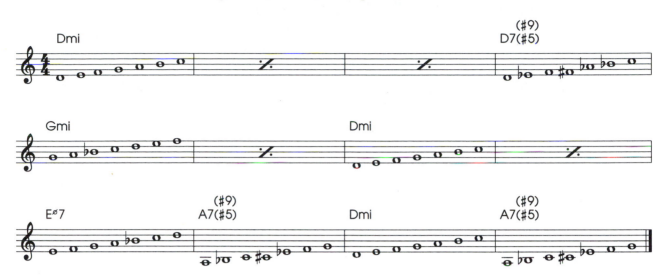

The exercises that follow the song explore some of these harmonic alternatives.

El Corazón

Treble Clef C Instruments
Latin

Scott Reeves

SOLOS

Repeat chords for solos. After solos,
D.C. al CODA (2nd time).

Treble Clef C Instruments—Exercises for "El Corazón"

1. Using the tonic minor pentatonic scale over the entire progression:

2. Using a descending minor pentatonic pattern over the entire progression:

3. Using a stepwise minor pentatonic pattern over the entire progression:

4. Using the dorian and superlocrian scales that fit each chord:

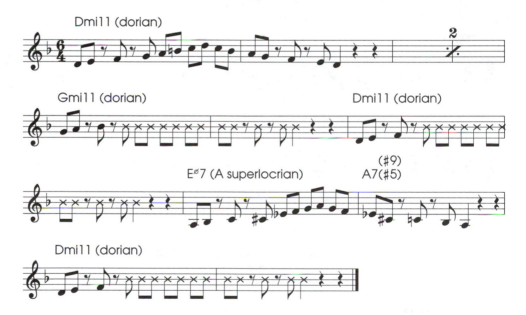

El Corazón

Repeat chords for solos. After solos,
D.C. al CODA (2nd time).

B♭ Instruments—Exercises for "El Corazón"

1. Using the tonic minor pentatonic scale over the entire progression:

2. Using a descending minor pentatonic pattern over the entire progression:

3. Using a stepwise minor pentatonic pattern over the entire progression:

4. Using the dorian and superlocrian scales that fit each chord:

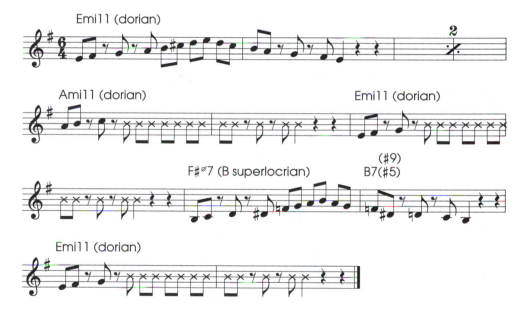

El Corazón

E♭ Instruments—Exercises for "El Corazón"

1. Using the tonic minor pentatonic scale over the entire progression:

2. Using a descending minor pentatonic pattern over the entire progression:

3. Using a stepwise minor pentatonic pattern over the entire progression:

4. Using the dorian and superlocrian scales that fit each chord:

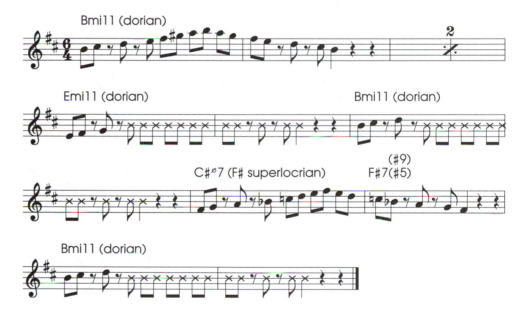

El Corazón

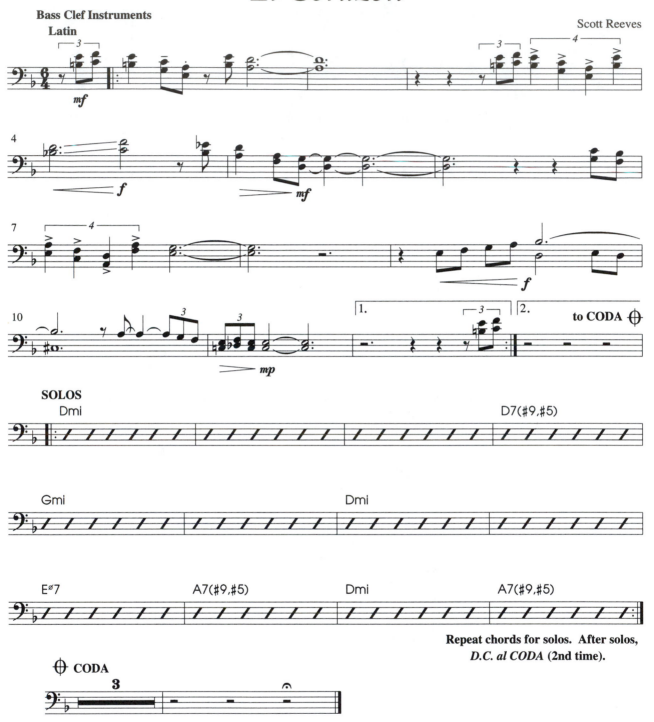

Repeat chords for solos. After solos,
D.C. al CODA **(2nd time).**

Bass Clef Instruments—Exercises for "El Corazón"

1. Using the tonic minor pentatonic scale over the entire progression:

2. Using a descending minor pentatonic pattern over the entire progression:

3. Using a stepwise minor pentatonic pattern over the entire progression:

4. Using the dorian and superlocrian scales that fit each chord:

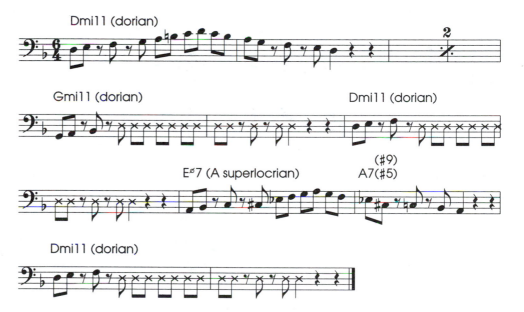

El Corazón

Scott Reeves

Piano/Guitar

Latin

**Repeat for solos. After solos,
D.C. al CODA (2nd time).**

El Corazón

Repeat for solos. After solos,
D.C. al CODA **(2nd time).**

CHAPTER

13

DIMINISHED SCALES AND DIMINISHED CHORDS

Diminished scales are unlike other scales in that they alternate half steps and whole steps. They contain eight notes exclusive of the octave and are also called *octatonic scales.* Diminished scales come in two forms—the *diminished (half step) scale,* which begins with a half step, and the *diminished (whole-step) scale,* which begins with a whole step:

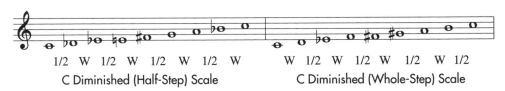

Both types of diminished scales are unique in that they cannot be transposed to more than three keys before they repeat themselves. For example, if you compare the C, E♭, F♯, and A diminished (whole-step) scales, you will notice that they contain the same notes, allowing for enharmonic spellings.

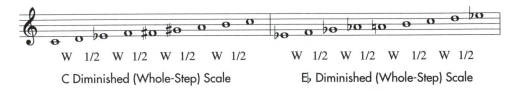

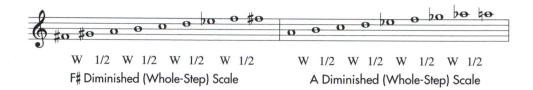

W 1/2 W 1/2 W 1/2 W 1/2   W 1/2 W 1/2 W 1/2 W 1/2
F♯ Diminished (Whole-Step) Scale   A Diminished (Whole-Step) Scale

Diminished scales have a symmetrical sound because of their alternation of half steps and whole steps and can be found in the music of twentieth-century classical composers such as Béla Bartók and Olivier Messiaen. Diminished scales became part of the jazz vocabulary after 1940 and were codified by George Russell in his jazz theory book, *The Lydian Chromatic Concept of Tonal Organization.*

The *diminished (whole-step) scale* can be thought of as being formed from the first four notes of a minor scale and the first four notes of the minor scale an augmented 4th above.

Diminished (whole-step) scales can be used when improvising over *fully diminished 7th chords,* which are the same as half-diminished chords with doubly lowered 7ths.

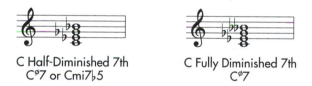

C Half-Diminished 7th   C Fully Diminished 7th
C°7 or Cmi7♭5   C°7

Fully diminished 7th chords contain a root, a minor 3rd, a diminished 5th, and a diminished 7th (which is enharmonic with the major 6th). Like diminished scales, diminished chords can be transposed to only three keys before they repeat themselves, allowing for enharmonic spellings.

C°7   E♭°7   F♯°7   A°7

Since all adjacent intervals in the fully diminished 7th chord are minor 3rds, the chord sounds the same in all inversions. It may also remind you of a train whistle or a sound overused by silent-movie composers.

Sometimes a major 7th is used in the chord instead of the diminished 7th. The *diminished/major 7th chord* has a strong "bite" but has more stability and color than the fully diminished 7th chord:

C° (MA7)

Diminished (half-step) scales are used when improvising on *dominant 7th chords* with raised or lowered 9ths. The diminished (half-step) scale contains a lowered 5th, but unlike the *superlocrian scale,* it does not have a raised 5th. With allowances for enharmonic spellings, we find the following chord tones in this scale:

Chord tones: root   ♭9   ♯9   3   ♭5   5   13   ♭7

Four different dominant 7th chords are found within each diminished (half-step) scale, allowing for enharmonic spellings. For example, the notes of the C7♭9, E♭7♭9, F♯7♭9, and A7♭9 chords are found within the C diminished (half-step) scale.

C7♭9   E♭7♭9   F♯7♭9   A7♭9

This implies that anything played over a C7♭9 chord will also sound good when played over the other three chords!

Both diminished (half-step) and superlocrian scales can be used over dominant 7th chords with altered 9ths. In general, diminished (half-step) scales are used more frequently in major keys, and superlocrian scales are the preferred choice in minor keys.

Some of the songs in which dominant 7th chords with altered 9ths figure prominently include "Barbara," "Blue in Green," "Hi-Fly," "Peace," and "Stella by Starlight." Fully diminished 7th chords can be found in compositions such as "Corcovado (Quiet Nights of Quiet Stars)," "How Insensitive," "I Remember Clifford," "Meditation," "Once I Loved," "Solitude," "Spring Is Here," and "Wave."[1] Both types of diminished scales work well over songs with ii–V progressions, even though some of the members of the ii chord are not found in either scale. When using diminished scales over ii–V progressions, you may use either the diminished (whole-step) scale based on the root of the ii chord or the diminished (half-step) scale based on the root of the V chord, since these two scales comprise the same notes.

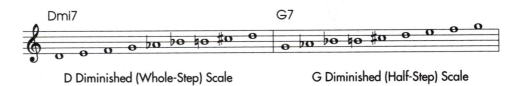

D Diminished (Whole-Step) Scale   G Diminished (Half-Step) Scale

Develop your ability to hear diminished 7th and altered dominant 7th chords by playing them on the piano.

[1]The music to these songs may be found in the following volumes of *A New Approach to Jazz Improvisation:* "Barbara" (Vol. 18), "Blue in Green" (Vol. 50), "Corcovado" (Vol. 31), "Hi-Fly" (Vol. 43), "How Insensitive" (Vol. 31), "I Remember Clifford" (Vol. 14), "Meditation" (Vol. 31), "Once I Loved" (Vol. 31), "Peace" (Vol. 17), "Solitude" (Vol. 12), "Spring Is Here" (Vol. 34), "Stella by Starlight" (Vol. 22), "Wave" (Vol. 31).

DIMINISHED SCALE WARM-UPS

Play the following exercises over the chord progression, using either a metronome, a live rhythm section, or the "ii–V–I Progression Diminished Scale Warm-Ups" play-along track on the companion CD. Play the written example over the first chord; then use your ear to play the exercise in the different keys indicated by the chord symbols. You will find it helpful to look at the chord progression instead of the exercises when playing in the remaining eleven keys. Pick a tempo at which you can effortlessly play each exercise, gradually moving on to more difficult exercises after you have mastered the easier ones.

Treble Clef C Instruments—Chord Progression

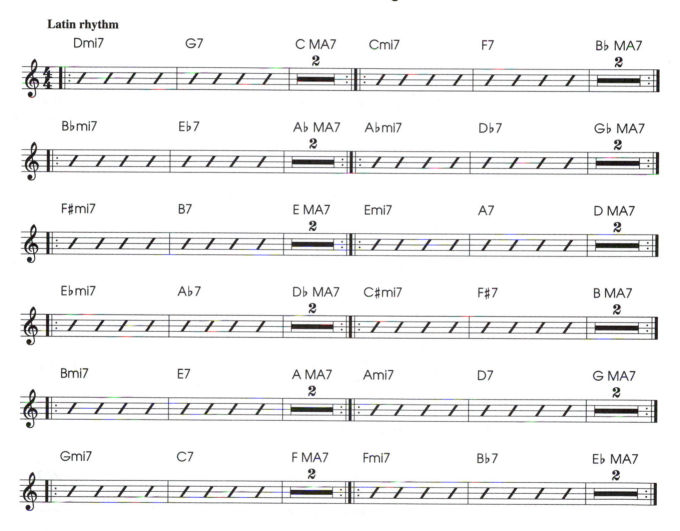

Treble Clef C Instruments—Beginning Exercises

1. The first five notes of the diminished (whole-step) scale:

2. The first five notes of the diminished (half-step) scale:

said 2
meant 3

Treble Clef C Instruments—Intermediate Exercises

3. The diminished (whole-step) scale:

4. The diminished (half-step) scale:

Treble Clef C Instruments—Advanced Exercises

5. The diminished (whole-step) scale in eighth notes:

6. A diminished (half-step) pattern:

B♭ Instruments—Chord Progression

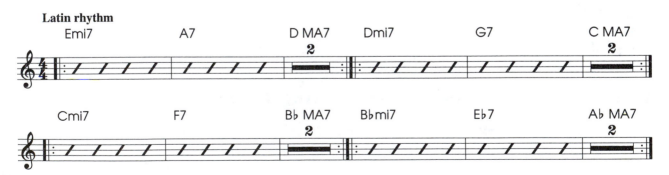

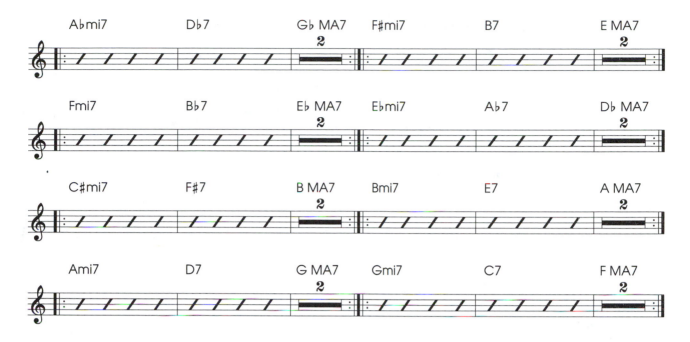

B♭ Instruments—Beginning Exercises

1. The first five notes of the diminished (whole-step) scale:

2. The first five notes of the diminished (half-step) scale:

B♭ Instruments—Intermediate Exercises

3. The diminished (whole-step) scale:

4. The diminished (half-step) scale:

B♭ Instruments—Advanced Exercises

5. The diminished (whole-step) scale in eighth notes:

6. A diminished (half-step) pattern:

E♭ Instruments—Chord Progression

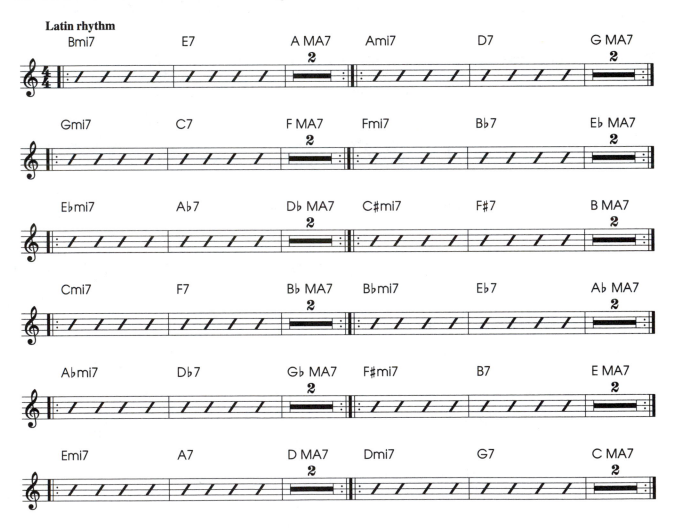

E♭ Instruments—Beginning Exercises

1. The first five notes of the diminished (whole-step) scale:

2. The first five notes of the diminished (half-step) scale:

E♭ Instruments—Intermediate Exercises

3. The diminished (whole-step) scale:

4. The diminished (half-step) scale:

E♭ Instruments—Advanced Exercises

5. The diminished (whole-step) scale in eighth notes:

6. A diminished (half-step) pattern:

Bass Clef Instruments—Chord Progression

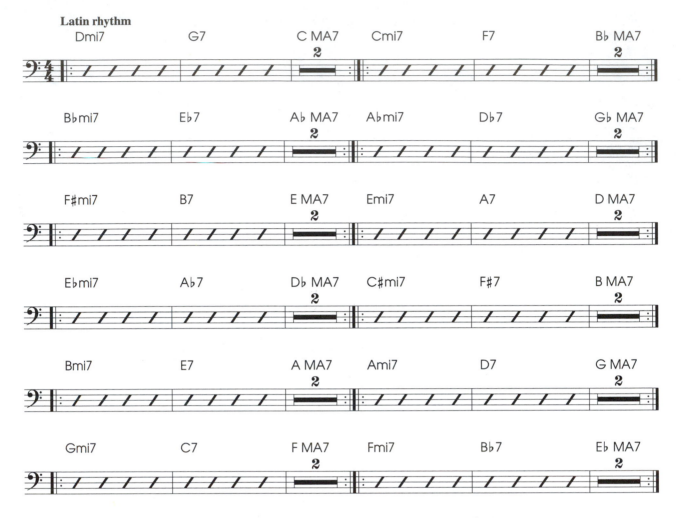

Bass Clef Instruments—Beginning Exercises

1. The first five notes of the diminished (whole-step) scale:

2. The first five notes of the diminished (half-step) scale:

Bass Clef Instruments—Intermediate Exercises

    3. The diminished (whole-step) scale:

    4. The diminished (half-step) scale:

Bass Clef Instruments—Advanced Exercises

    5. The diminished (whole-step) scale in eighth notes:

    6. A diminished (half-step) pattern:

All Instruments—Improvisation Exercises

    1. Improvise on diminished scales in all keys, using a live rhythm section or the "ii–V–I Progressions and Diminished Scale Warm-Ups" play-along track on the companion CD.

    2. Make up your own exercises and melodic ideas based on diminished scales.

ℐMPROVISING ON DIMINISHED SCALES

"Nuthouse" is a composition in which diminished scales figure prominently in the melody and harmonic implications. Practice and improvise on the song, using either a metronome, a live rhythm section, or the "Nuthouse" play-along track on the companion CD. (On the CD, the chord progression is played six times.)

"Nuthouse" is based on the chord progression to a Cole Porter composition, "What Is This Thing Called Love?"[2] It is cast in a 32-bar AABA form; the A section centers on the concert keys of F minor and C major, and the B section begins in B♭ major and returns to the starting key. The key centers and optional related chords (enclosed in parentheses) are shown in this analysis:

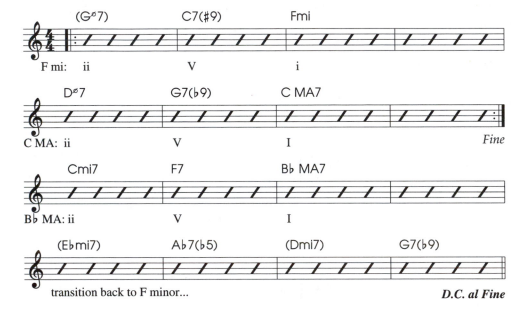

The chord progression can be simplified by reducing it to the following tonal areas:

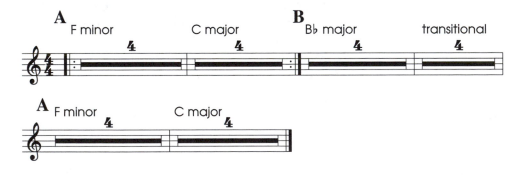

---

[2]Cole Porter, "What Is This Thing Called Love?" copyright 1929, renewed by Warner Brothers, Inc.

There are a couple of options with regard to the scales that color these chords. Over the first chord, the superlocrian scale would normally be the first choice, but the diminished (half-step) scale may also be used. During the major ii–V's dorian and mixolydian scales may be used to create an "inside" sound, whereas diminished scales will bring out the sound of the chord alterations.

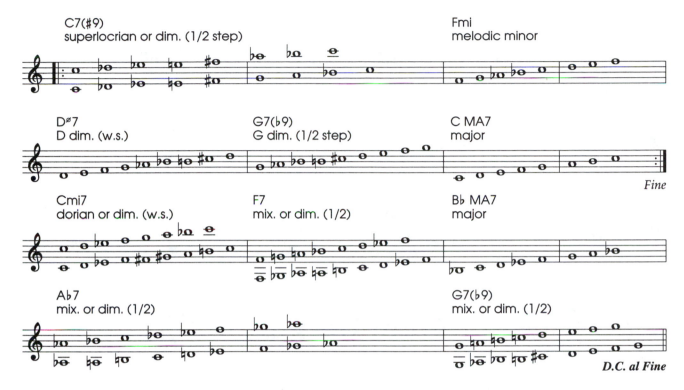

Within the melody of the song, diminished scales are found in measures 14, 17–18, 27–28, 61, 66, and 70, and superlocrian scales are used in measures 5–6, 10, 22, 29–30, 34, and 57–58 and in the coda.

The exercises that follow the song will help you gain facility in using diminished scales over this progression.

Nuthouse

Treble Clef C Instruments
Swing

Scott Reeves

Treble Clef C Instruments—Exercises for "Nuthouse"

1. Using the descending diminished (half-step) scale over the ii–V progressions:

2. Using the minor or half-diminished 7th arpeggio over the ii chords and the 3-5-♭7-♭9 over the V chords:

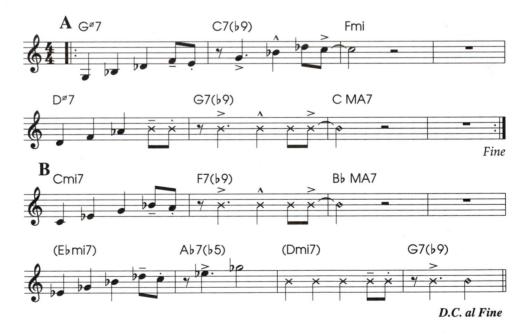

3. Using the ascending diminished (whole-step) scale over the ii–V progressions:

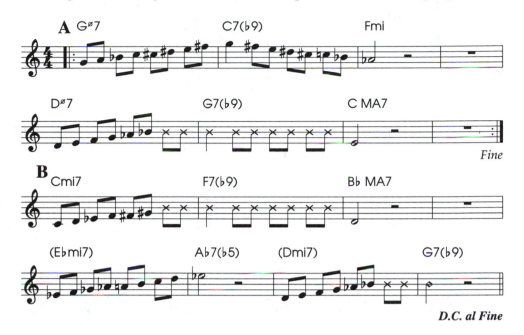

Nuthouse

B♭ Instruments—Exercises for "Nuthouse"

1. Using the descending diminished (half-step) scale over the ii–V progressions:

2. Using the minor or half-diminished 7th arpeggio over the ii chords and the 3-5-♭7-♭9 over the V chords:

3. Using the ascending diminished (whole-step) scale over the ii–V progressions:

Fine

D.C. al Fine

Nuthouse

266

E♭ Instruments—Exercises for "Nuthouse"

1. Using the descending diminished (half-step) scale over the ii–V progressions:

2. Using the minor or half-diminished 7th arpeggio over the ii chords and the 3-5-♭7-♭9 over the V chords:

3. Using the ascending diminished (whole-step) scale over the ii–V progressions:

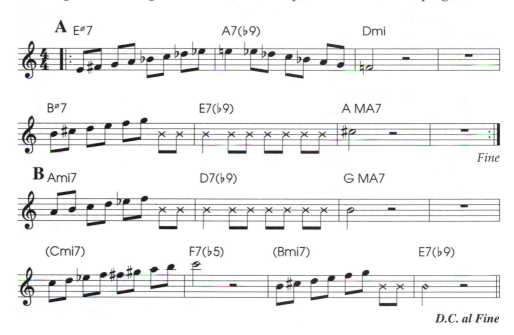

Nuthouse

Bass Clef Instruments
Swing

Scott Reeves

Bass Clef Instruments—Exercises for "Nuthouse"

1. Using the descending diminished (half-step) scale over the ii–V progressions:

2. Using the minor or half-diminished 7th arpeggio over the ii chords and the 3-5-♭7-♭9 over the V chords:

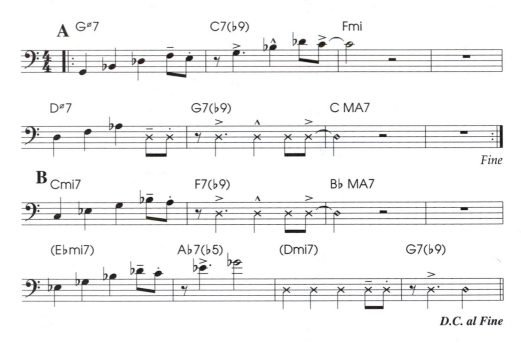

3. Using the ascending diminished (whole-step) scale over the ii–V progressions:

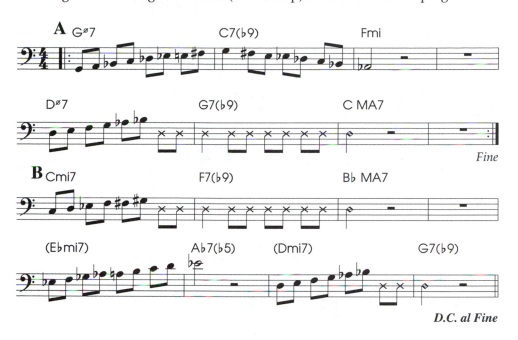

Fine

D.C. al Fine

Nuthouse

Piano/Guitar
Swing

Scott Reeves

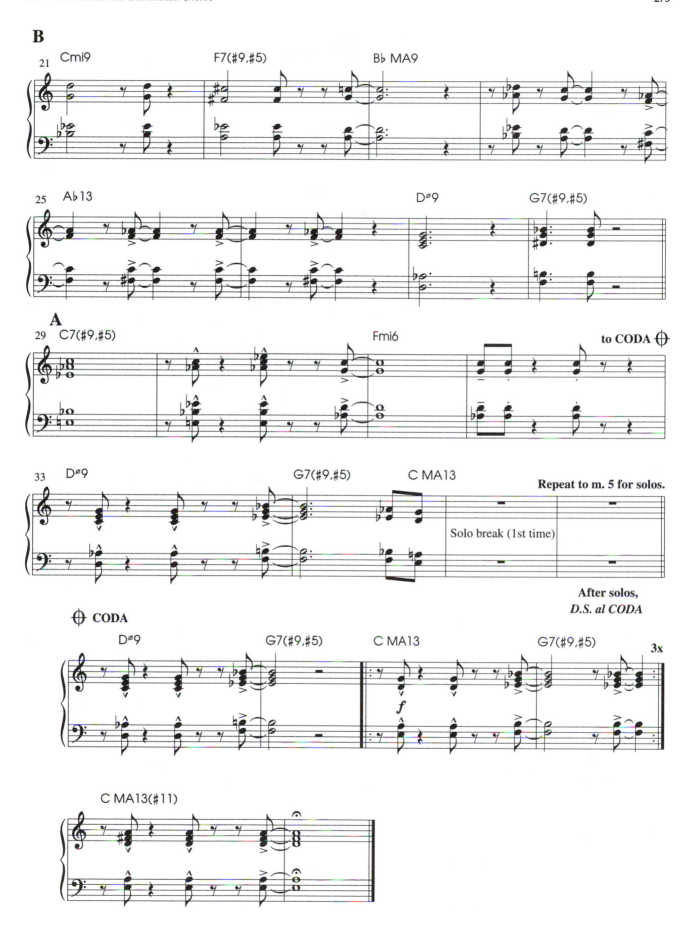

Nuthouse

Bass
Swing

Scott Reeves

Solo break—1st time   **Repeat to m. 5 for solos**
(walk during the A sections
After solos, *D.S. al CODA*

The conscious mind is like the Armed Forces.
You need the military to protect the country,
but you don't want the generals to take over
the government.

—pianist Kenny Werner, discussing the
role of conscious thought during
the act of improvisation

CHAPTER

14

BASIC MUSIC THEORY

CLEFS

Clef signs are used to indicate the names of the lines and spaces on the staff. The *treble clef,* or *G clef,* curves around to end on the second line, indicating the position of G. The *bass clef,* or *F clef,* starts on the fourth line, indicating the position of F. Two less commonly used clefs, the *alto clef* and the *tenor clef,* indicate where middle C is found and are sometimes called *C clefs.* When notes occur above or below the staff, *ledger lines* are used to extend the staff. To learn the clefs, memorize the names of the lines and spaces. In treble clef, the spaces spell "F-A-C-E"; the lines are E-G-B-D-F ("Every Good Boy Does Fine"). The spaces in bass clef are A-C-E-G ("All Cows Eat Grass"); the lines are G-B-D-F-A ("Good Boys Do Fine Always").

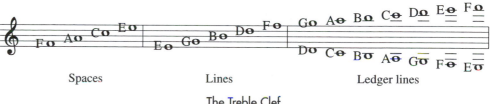

Spaces   Lines   Ledger lines

The Treble Clef

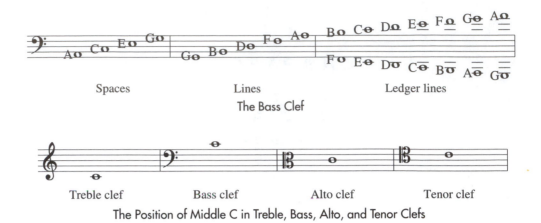

Spaces   Lines   Ledger lines

The Bass Clef

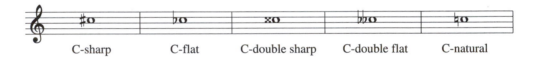

Treble clef   Bass clef   Alto clef   Tenor clef

The Position of Middle C in Treble, Bass, Alto, and Tenor Clefs

ACCIDENTALS

Accidentals are used to raise or lower pitches. A sharp raises a note one half step; a flat lowers a note one half step. A double sharp raises a note two half steps; a double flat lowers a note two half steps. A natural sign cancels all previous accidentals. Accidentals are written just before the note they affect and are written on the same line or space as the note.

C-sharp   C-flat   C-double sharp   C-double flat   C-natural

INTERVALS

Intervals are the building blocks of music. All scales, melodies, and chords are made up of intervals. Therefore, it is important to become familiar with intervals so that you can write them and play them on your instrument.

An interval consists of two notes. These notes can occur one after the other (a *melodic interval*) or simultaneously (a *harmonic interval*). Interval names consist of two parts: a prefix (such as major, minor, perfect, augmented, or diminished), followed by a number indicating the distance between the two notes. If that number is less than 8, the interval is a *simple interval*. If the number is 8 (referred to as an *octave*) or more, the interval is a *compound interval*. Below are some examples of simple and compound intervals.

Perfect 5th   Minor 9th   Major 6th   Augmented 11th
(simple)   (compound)   (simple)   (compound)

Simple intervals have *compound equivalents.* For example, a 2nd plus an octave is called a 9th, a 4th plus an octave is called an 11th, and a 6th plus an octave is called a 13th.

To find the numerical part of the name, simply count the number of lines and spaces between the two notes, being sure to count the first note as 1. For example, to identify this interval, count the lines and spaces from F up to C:

To identify descending melodic intervals, simply count the lines and spaces downward:

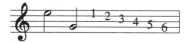

Exercise 1

Fill in the numerical part of the following intervals.

Major _____   Minor _____   Perfect _____   Minor _____   Perfect _____

There are two different ways to determine the prefix portion of the name of an interval. The first method involves counting the number of half steps between the two notes. Use the following table if you choose to use this approach, being sure to count the first note as 1.

Number of Half Steps Between Notes	Interval Name (to the 13th)	Abbreviation
None	Perfect unison	P1
One	Augmented unison or minor 2nd	+1 mi 2
Two	Major 2nd or diminished 3rd	MA 2 °3
Three	Augmented 2nd or minor 3rd	+2 mi 3
Four	Major 3rd or diminished 4th	MA 3 °4
Five	Augmented 3rd or perfect 4th	+3 P4
Six	Augmented 4th or diminished 5th	+4 °5

Number of Half Steps Between Notes	Interval Name (to the 13th)	Abbreviation
Seven	Perfect 5th or diminished 6th	P5 °6
Eight	Augmented 5th or minor 6th	+5 ♭6
Nine	Major 6th or diminished 7th	MA 6 °7
Ten	Augmented 6th or minor 7th	+6 mi7
Eleven	Major 7th or diminished octave	MA7 °8
Twelve	Perfect octave	P8
Thirteen	Augmented octave or minor 9th	+8 ♭9
Fourteen	Major 9th or diminished 10th	MA 9 °10
Fifteen	Augmented 9th or minor 10th	+9 ♭10
Sixteen	Major 10th or diminished 11th	MA 10 °11
Seventeen	Augmented 10th or perfect 11th	+10 P 11
Eighteen	Augmented 11th or diminished 12th	+11 °12
Nineteen	Perfect 12th or diminished 13th	P 12 °13
Twenty	Augmented 12th or minor 13th	+12 ♭13
Twenty-one	Major 13th	MA 13

In looking over this list, you may have noticed that intervals have more than one name, such as augmented 2nd and minor 3rd. Although these intervals sound the same and have an identical number of half steps, they are written differently. When two notes, intervals, or chords sound the same but are spelled differently, they are called *enharmonic*. (One such enharmonic interval, the augmented 4th/diminished 5th, has a nickname: the *tritone*.)

You may have noticed also that 2nds, 3rds, 6ths, and 7ths and their compound equivalents have different prefixes from unisons, 4ths, and 5ths and their compound equivalents. In every major scale, the interval from the first note to the rest of the notes in the scale is as follows:

First note of the scale to itself = perfect unison

First note of the scale up to the second note = major 2nd

First note of the scale up to the third note = major 3rd

First note of the scale up to the fourth note = perfect 4th

First note of the scale up to the fifth note = perfect 5th

First note of the scale up to the sixth note = major 6th

First note of the scale up to the seventh note = major 7th

Therefore, unisons, 4ths, and 5ths and their compound equivalents (octaves, 11ths, and 12ths) are called *perfect* if they are unchanged from the way they occur in a major scale. If these intervals are contracted by one half step, they are called *diminished*. If they are expanded by one half step, they are called *augmented*. In contrast, the 2nds, 3rds, 6ths, and 7ths and their compound equivalents are called *major* if they are unchanged from the way they appear in the major scale. If these intervals are contracted by one half step, they are called *minor*. If they are expanded one half step, they are called *augmented*. If they are contracted by two half steps (without changing the numerical part of the name), they are called *diminished*.

Intervals	Unchanged from Major Scale	Contracted Half Step	Contracted Two Half Steps	Expanded Half Step
Unisons, 4ths, 5ths, octaves, 11ths, 12ths	are called "perfect"	are called "diminished"	are called "doubly diminished"	are called "augmented"
2nds, 3rds, 6ths, 7ths, 9ths, 10ths, 13ths	are called "major"	are called "minor"	are called "diminished"	are called "augmented"

A second method of determining the prefix name of an interval uses the lower note of the interval as the first note of a major scale, then compares that interval with the intervals found in a major scale. For example, to find the name of this interval:

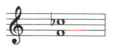

compare it with the notes in an F major scale:

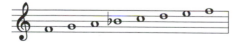

Notice that the fifth note of the scale is a C-natural. That tells you that F to C is a perfect 5th. Since C♭ is one half step below C-natural, the interval from F to C♭ is a diminished 5th.

To determine the name of this interval:

compare it with an F major scale (use the lower note of the interval as the first note of the scale, even if it comes second in a melodic interval):

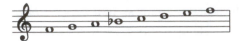

Since F to D is a major 6th, F to D♯ must be an augmented 6th.

   If the lower note of the interval forms a scale that is difficult to visualize (such as E♯), transpose the interval to an easier key a half step away. To find the name of this interval:

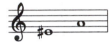

transpose the interval down a half step:

Then think of the notes in an E major scale:

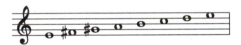

Because A is the fourth note in the scale, the interval from E to A must be a perfect 4th. Since this distance has been contracted by a half step, the intervals from E to A♭ and E♯ to A must be diminished 4ths.

Exercise 2

Using either the table of half steps or the major-scale approach, write the following intervals above the given note.

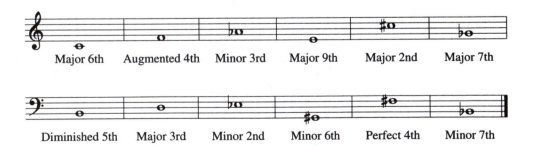

Exercise 3

Write the complete name of each interval (prefix and number) in the space provided.

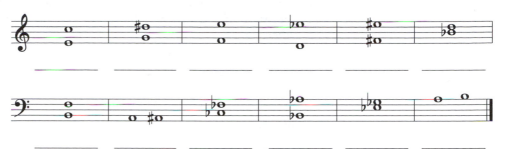

_____ _____ _____ _____ _____ _____

_____ _____ _____ _____ _____ _____

Sometimes it is easier to write descending intervals by using *interval inversion.* To invert an interval, transpose the upper note down an octave so that it is below the lower note:

inverts to

When inverted, perfect intervals are still called perfect, major intervals become minor, and augmented intervals become diminished. The numerical portion of the interval and its inversion will total 9 when added together. For instance, a perfect 5th inverts to a perfect 4th (5 + 4 = 9), a major 3rd inverts to a minor 6th, and a diminished 7th inverts to an augmented 2nd. Using this method, you may write a descending minor 7th by writing an ascending major 2nd and putting the top note down an octave:

inverts to

Major 2nd   Minor 7th

This method is particularly helpful when writing descending intervals larger than a 4th.

Exercise 4

Write the following intervals *below* the given note.

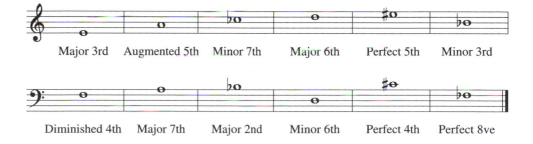

Major 3rd   Augmented 5th   Minor 7th   Major 6th   Perfect 5th   Minor 3rd

Diminished 4th   Major 7th   Major 2nd   Minor 6th   Perfect 4th   Perfect 8ve

Although it is important for a "literate" musician to be able to write and identify intervals, it is even more important for an improvisor to learn to recognize them by their sound. Each interval has its own characteristic sound, or "color," which identifies it. You can also learn to recognize an interval by relating it to the opening interval of a familiar song. Below is a partial list of songs and the intervals with which they begin.

Beginning Interval	Songs
Ascending minor 2nd	"Silver Bells"
Ascending major 2nd	"Happy Birthday" (2nd-to-3rd note); "Silent Night"
Ascending minor 3rd	"Greensleeves"; "O Come, O Come, Emmanuel"
Ascending major 3rd	"When the Saints Go Marching In"
Ascending perfect 4th	"Here Comes the Bride"
Ascending augmented 4th/diminished 5th	"Maria" (from *West Side Story*)
Ascending perfect 5th	Theme from *Star Wars*; "Twinkle, Twinkle, Little Star"
Ascending minor 6th	Theme from "Lassie"; "Morning of the Carnival"
Ascending major 6th	"Bring Back My Bonnie to Me"; "Take the 'A' Train"
Ascending minor 7th	"Somewhere" (from *West Side Story*); theme from original "Star Trek" series
Ascending major 7th	Theme from "Fantasy Island"
Ascending perfect 8ve	"Over the Rainbow"
Descending minor 2nd	"Joy to the World"
Descending major 2nd	"Three Blind Mice"
Descending minor 3rd	"The Star-Spangled Banner"
Descending major 3rd	"Swing Low, Sweet Chariot"
Descending perfect 4th	"All of Me"
Descending augmented 4th	"Blue Seven"
Descending perfect 5th	"Feelings"
Descending minor 6th	Theme from *Love Story*
Descending major 6th	"Over There"; "Bye-Bye Blues"; "Nobody Knows the Trouble I've Seen"
Descending minor 7th	"Watermelon Man"
Descending major 7th	"I Love You"
Descending perfect 8ve	"Willow Weep for Me"

Exercise 5

Sing each interval, paying attention to the unique color of each.

Exercise 6

Have your teacher or another musician play a series of random intervals. On your instrument, play what you have just heard.

Tonal Gravity

Melodies are made up of a series of intervals. When transcribing or playing melodies by ear, you can relate each interval to familiar songs or try to hear each note in relationship to the *tonic*. The tonic is the first note of the scale; in *tonal music* (music that has a key), it is the pitch to which all other notes eventually resolve. The tonic can be viewed as having *tonal gravity,* which pulls on all the other pitches to a greater or lesser extent. The fifth note of the scale is called the *dominant* and has a certain amount of tonal gravity, though less than the tonic. Because of this, it is easy to confuse the dominant with the tonic. The dominant, however, has a strong tendency to resolve down a perfect 5th or up a perfect 4th to the tonic. This resolution from dominant to tonic is the strongest movement in tonal music and is the ultimate goal of most chord progressions. All other notes in the scale can be heard in relationship to how strongly they wish to resolve to either the dominant or the tonic, as indicated by the following table.

Scale Degree	Formal Name	Resolves To	Comments
1	Tonic	——	Strongest note in the tonal gravity system.
2	Supertonic	Tonic	Very unstable. Can also move upward to the mediant.
3	Mediant	Tonic	Third strongest note in the tonal gravity system.
4	Subdominant	Mediant	Very unstable. Occasionally moves upward to the dominant.
5	Dominant	Tonic	Second strongest note in the tonal gravity system. A temporary "resting" place before resolving to the tonic.
6	Submediant	Dominant	Unstable.
7	Leading tone	Tonic	The most unstable note in the tonal gravity system. It is strongly pulled up by the tonic.

By keeping the sound of the tonic in your head as a reference note, you can determine all other pitches by their degree of tension and need to resolve to the tonic, the mediant, or the dominant.

Exercise 7

Have your teacher or another musician play some short melodies. Using either reference intervals from familiar songs or the tonal gravity system, write down or play what you have just heard.

KEY SIGNATURES

Key signatures are used to avoid writing *accidentals* (sharps, flats, naturals, double flats, and double sharps) every time they occur. Key signatures appear at the beginning of a composition, between the clef sign and the time signature, and are valid for the entire piece unless subsequent accidentals contradict them. When accidentals occur elsewhere in the piece, they affect only the measure in which they occur.

There is an easy way to memorize key signatures. For major keys with flats (F, B♭, E♭, A♭, D♭, G♭, C♭), the name of the key is the same as the second-to-last accidental in the key signature, with the exception of the key of F, which has only one flat. Therefore, all you need to do is memorize the order of flats: B♭, E♭, A♭, D♭, G♭, C♭, and F♭.

Order of Flats

When you wish to write the key signature of A♭, simply write the flats in this order until you arrive at A♭, then add one more flat beyond that to the key signature. Notice that by convention, the accidentals are written on the lines and spaces that correspond to specific octaves.

For major keys with sharps (G, D, A, E, B, F♯, C♯), the name of the key is one half step higher than the last sharp. To write a key signature in a sharp key, write the sharps in the order in which they occur. F♯, C♯, G♯, D♯, A♯, E♯, and B♯.

Order of Sharps

Stop writing accidentals when you get to the sharp that is one half step below the name of the key.

Minor keys have the same key signature as major keys a minor 3rd higher. For example, E minor and G major have the same key signature and are referred to as the *relative minor* and the *relative major* of each other. To remember that the minor key is a minor 3rd below the major key, think of minor keys as being "sad" or "*down* in feeling" and therefore *down* a minor 3rd from major.

You can also learn major and minor key signatures by memorizing the *Circle of Fourths/Fifths.* As you move clockwise around the cycle, each key is a perfect 4th higher than the previous key and adds one flat to the key signature. As you move counterclockwise, each key is a perfect 5th above the previous key and adds one sharp to the key signature.

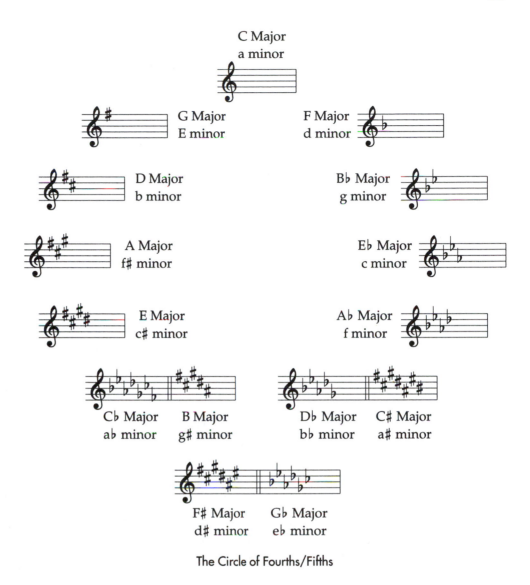

The Circle of Fourths/Fifths

Exercise 8

Without looking at the Circle of Fourths/Fifths, write the following key signatures. (When writing minor key signatures, you may find it helpful to first determine the key signature of the relative major.)

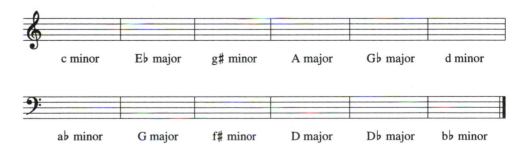

Exercise 9

Without looking at the Circle of Fourths/Fifths, identify the following key signatures.

_____ major   _____ minor   _____ minor   _____ major   _____ major   _____ minor

---

TIME SIGNATURES

The time signature follows the clef sign and the key signature at the beginning of a composition and also occurs whenever the meter changes during the piece. The top number in the time signature indicates the number of beats per measure, and the bottom number indicates what type of note gets one beat. For example, in 3/4 meter, the 3 indicates three beats per measure, and the 4 tells you that a quarter note receives one beat. In 6/8 meter, the 6 indicates six beats to the measure, and the 8 indicates that the eighth note gets one beat.

Time signatures are classified as *simple* or *compound*. In simple meters, such as 2/4, 3/4, and 4/4, the beats can be *subdivided* in half (as if you were counting "ONE-and-TWO-and-THREE-and-FOUR-and"). In compound meters, such as 6/8, 9/8, and 12/8, each grouping of three beats is felt as one large beat (as if you were counting "ONE-two-three-FOUR-five-six-SEVEN-eight-nine-TEN-eleven-twelve"). Typically, simple meters have one, two, three, or four beats per measure, and compound meters contain six, nine, or twelve beats to the bar. Occasionally, we find a composition in which the number of beats per measure is not divisible by 2 or 3, such as 5/4 or 7/4. These time signatures are called *asymmetrical*. In jazz, the best known example of a song with an asymmetrical meter is Paul Desmond's "Take Five," which is in 5/4 meter.

In the notation of rhythms in simple meters, the notes are *tied* or *beamed* so that all primary beats can be seen; in compound meters, the notes are tied or beamed so that each grouping of three beats is visible. Beams are used to connect notes within a beat, and ties are used for notes that extend across a beat. The following are examples of incorrectly and correctly notated simple and compound meters:

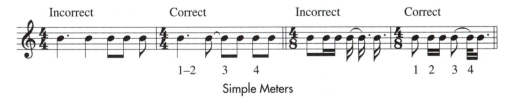

Simple Meters

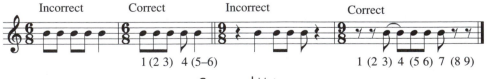

Compound Meters

Exercise 10

Rewrite the following incorrect rhythms. Be sure to show the primary beats in simple meters and groupings of threes in compound meters.

CHAPTER
15

JAZZ THEORY

Except in certain free jazz styles, the jazz musician improvises on the *melody*, the *form*, and the *chord progression* of a song. The performer must know this "blueprint" so thoroughly that he or she does not have to consciously think about it. To get to this level of intimacy with a song, it can be helpful to develop an understanding of the theoretical basis of jazz.

SCALES AND MODAL FAMILIES

An improvisor spontaneously makes up melodies based on the chord progression of the tune. Therefore, the jazz artist has to be able to pick out notes that fit the underlying chords. In addition to the chord tones, the scales that accompany these chords may be used as the raw materials for improvisation. A basic tenet of jazz theory is that for every chord, there is at least one scale that best colors it. This chapter presents an overview of many of the scales or *modes* used by jazz musicians. Bear in mind that an intellectual understanding of a scale does not guarantee that you will be able to improvise on it in a creative manner. To create interesting music with a scale, you must practice the scale until it becomes an automatic reflex.

Many of the modes are derived from one "parent" scale and belong to the same *modal family*. There are seven modes in the *major scale family*, seven in the *melodic minor family* (five of which are commonly used), two in the *diminished scale family*, five in the *major pentatonic family* (of which two are used), six in the *blues scale* (of which only one is used), and one in the *whole-tone scale*.

The following modes result from starting on each note in the *major scale* and continuing upward for one octave.

Scale Degree	Name of Mode	Use and Sound Quality
1st note	Major scale	Used over major 7th chords; has a "pretty" sound
2nd note	Dorian mode	Used over minor 7th chords in a ii–V–I progression
3rd note	Phrygian mode	Used over minor chords; has a "Spanish" sound
4th note	Lydian mode	Used over major 7th and major 7♯11 chords; has an exotic quality
5th note	Mixolydian mode	Used over unaltered dominant 7th chords; has a "jazzy" or "bluesy" quality
6th note	Aeolian mode	Used over tonic minor chords; has a sad quality
7th note	Locrian mode	Used over half-diminished chords; has an unresolved quality because of its lack of a perfect 5th

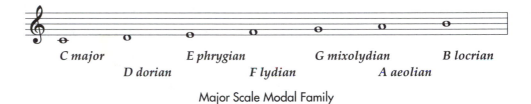

C major *D dorian* *E phrygian* *F lydian* *G mixolydian* *A aeolian* *B locrian*

Major Scale Modal Family

The following modes result from forming a scale on each note in the *ascending melodic minor scale.* (The modes built on the second and the fifth notes are not typically used in jazz improvisation.)

Scale Degree	Name of Mode	Use and Sound Quality
1st note	Melodic minor	Used over minor chords with major 7ths
3rd note	Lydian augmented	Used over major 7♯5 chords; has an extremely exotic quality
4th note	Lydian dominant	Used over dominant 9♯11 chords; has a color favored by some Brazilian musicians
6th note	Locrian ♯2	Used over half-diminished 7th chords; has an unresolved quality
7th note	Superlocrian	Used over dominant 7th chords with altered 9ths and 5ths; along with the melodic minor, the most commonly used mode in this family

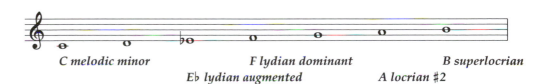

C melodic minor *Eb lydian augmented* *F lydian dominant* *A locrian ♯2* *B superlocrian*

Melodic Minor Modal Family

Because *diminished scales* alternate half steps and whole steps, only two modes occur: the *diminished (whole-step) mode*, which begins with a whole step, and the *diminished (half-step) mode*, which begins with a half step.

Scale Degree	Name of Scale	Use and Sound Quality
1st, 3rd, 5th, 7th notes	Diminished (whole-step)	Used over diminished 7th chords or ii chords in a major or minor ii–V–I progression
2nd, 4th, 6th, 8th notes	Diminished (half-step)	Used over dominant 7th chords with altered 9ths

Diminished scales have eight notes, not inclusive of the octave, and are sometimes called *octatonic* scales.

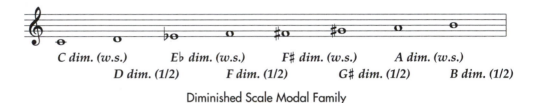

C dim. (w.s.)   Eb dim. (w.s.)   F# dim. (w.s.)   A dim. (w.s.)
  D dim. (1/2)   F dim. (1/2)   G# dim. (1/2)   B dim. (1/2)

Diminished Scale Modal Family

There are many types of *pentatonic scales*; the ones most commonly used by jazz musicians are the *major and minor pentatonic modes.*

Scale Degree	Name of Scale	Use and Sound Quality
1st note	Major pentatonic	Used over major or dominant 7th chords, particularly in modal tunes; has a bright, open quality
5th note	Minor pentatonic	Used over minor 7th chords, particularly in modal tunes; has a dark, "bluesy" feeling

C major pentatonic   A minor pentatonic

Major Pentatonic Modes

The *blues scale* is used only in its first mode.

C Blues Scale

It has a "bluesy" quality and can be used over both minor 7th and dominant 7th chords.

Because the *whole-tone scale* consists entirely of whole steps, each mode in the parent scale will also be a whole-tone scale.

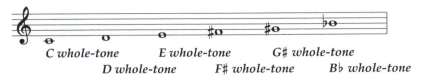

C whole-tone   E whole-tone   G# whole-tone
        D whole-tone   F# whole-tone   Bb whole-tone

Whole-Tone Scale

The whole-tone scale is used over augmented triads or dominant 7th chords with altered 5ths. Its lack of half steps gives it a very unusual color. It is favored by composers such as Claude Debussy and Thelonious Monk.

Exercise 1

Sing and play each of the previous modes, paying attention to their colors and moods.

Exercise 2

On a separate piece of paper, transpose the major scale, the melodic minor scale, the diminished scale, the blues scale, and the whole-tone scale to a key other than C. Then write out the remaining six modes in the major scale family and the remaining four modes in the melodic minor family.

CHORDS

Chords are defined as three or more notes sounded simultaneously. Sounding the notes in a chord one at a time produces a *chord arpeggio*. *Triads* are three-note chords consisting of a *root* (the lowest note), a 3rd, and a 5th. *Seventh chords* are made up of four notes, *ninth chords* contain five notes, *eleventh chords* have six notes, and *thirteenth chords* consist of seven notes. Each additional chord tone adds color and tension to the harmony.

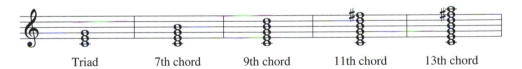

Triad   7th chord   9th chord   11th chord   13th chord

In early jazz, the harmonic instruments usually played triads or triads with added 6ths. During the swing era of the 1930s, 7th chords were the norm. The bebop style of the '40s added altered 5ths and 9ths to chords, and 11ths and 13ths were common in the '50s and '60s. Typically, most jazz chords are referred to as 7th chords, but that does not preclude the player from adding notes beyond the 7th (called *extensions*) to the chord.

Chords are usually stacked in intervals of 3rds and are referred to as *tertian voicings*. When chords are stacked in intervals of 4ths, they are known as *quartal voicings*. Quartal voicings are particularly common in modal compositions such as Miles Davis's "So What" as well as in much of John Coltrane's work from 1960 to 1965.

Quartal Voicing

Seventh chords are categorized according to the type of intervals used to build them. *Major 7th chords* contain a root, a major 3rd, a perfect 5th, and a major 7th. They can be extended by adding a major 9th, an augmented 11th, and a major 13th. Major 7th chords typically sound "pretty" or "lush" when played.

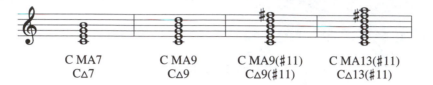

| C MA7 | C MA9 | C MA9(♯11) | C MA13(♯11) |
| C△7 | C△9 | C△9(♯11) | C△13(♯11) |

Dominant 7th chords contain a root, a major 3rd, a perfect 5th, and a minor 7th. Extensions may include a major 9th, an augmented 11th (if used in conjunction with the 3rd), a perfect 11th (if used in place of the 3rd—known as a *sus. 4 chord*), and a major 13th. Dominant chords have a "jazzy" or "biting" quality.

C7   C9   C9(♯11)   C9(sus.4)   C13(♯11)

The 5th of the major 7th or the dominant 7th chord can be altered by raising or lowering it a half step; the 9th of the dominant 7th chord can also be altered by raising or lowering it a half step.

C MA7(♭5)   C MA7(♯5)   C7(♭5)   C7(♯5)   C7(♭9)   C7(♯5,♯9)

Minor 7th chords contain a root, a minor 3rd, a perfect 5th, and a minor 7th. These chords can be extended by adding a major 9th, a perfect 11th, and a major 13th. (Notice that minor 9th and minor 13th chords contain *major* 9ths and *major* 13ths.) Minor 7th chords have a mellow or "bluesy" character.

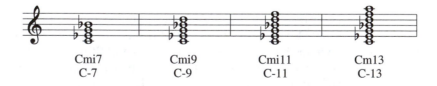

| Cmi7 | Cmi9 | Cmi11 | Cm13 |
| C-7 | C-9 | C-11 | C-13 |

In a minor key, a minor triad with a major 7th is occasionally used.

Cmi/MA7
C-(△7)

The *minor/major 7th chord* sounds like a minor 7th chord with more "bite" and does not have a tendency to progress to a dominant 7th chord.

Major, minor, and dominant 7th chords are the most commonly used chords in jazz, but *half-diminished 7th chords* (consisting of a root, a minor 3rd, a diminished 5th, and a minor 7th) and *fully diminished 7th chords* (consisting of a root, a minor 3rd, a diminished 5th, and a diminished 7th) are occasionally encountered. Extensions to the half-diminished chord include the major 9th and the perfect 11th. Fully diminished chords can be extended by adding all remaining notes in the diminished scale, usually in the form of a *doubly diminished* voicing.

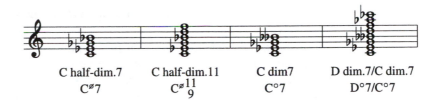

Half-diminished chords have an "unresolved" quality and want to progress up a perfect 4th to an altered dominant chord. Fully diminished 7th chords are very unstable and usually move up a half step to a more stable chord. The following chart summarizes these different chord types.

Chord Type	Intervallic Composition	Sound/Color
Major 7th	Root-MA3-P5-MA7	Pretty, lush, warm, yellow
Dominant 7th	Root-MA3-P5-mi7	Jazzy, biting, strong, red
Minor 7th	Root-mi3-P5-mi7	Mellow, introspective, blue
Half-diminished 7th	Root-mi3-dim.5-mi7	Unstable
Fully diminished 7th	Root-mi3-dim.5-dim.7	Very unstable, vague

E x e r c i s e   3

Write the following chords, being sure to use the correct intervals above the root.

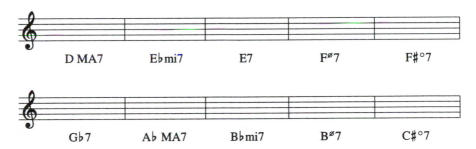

DIATONIC CHORDS

Chords are derived from scales by building a chord on every other note in the scale. Chords taken from the same scale are known as *diatonic chords.*

Diatonic Chords in the Major Scale

Each of these chords is labeled with the roman numeral that corresponds to its position within the scale. (Uppercase numerals are used for major and dominant 7th chords, lowercase numerals for minor and diminished 7th chords.) Each chord is also given the same formal name as the note on which it is built: I = tonic, ii = supertonic, iii = mediant, IV = subdominant, V = dominant, vi = submediant, vii = leading tone, and ♭VII = subtonic.

In *major keys*, the I and IV chords are major 7th chords; the ii, iii, and vi chords are minor 7th chords; the V chord is a dominant 7th chord; and the vii chord is a half-diminished 7th chord. In *minor keys*, the i chord may be either a minor 7th or a minor/major 7th chord; the ii chord is a half-diminished 7th chord; the III and VI chords are major 7th chords; the iv chord is usually a minor 7th chord; and the V chord is normally a dominant 7th chord. The vii chord is usually a fully diminished 7th chord built on the leading tone, but occasionally it occurs as a major or dominant 7th chord built on the lowered seventh (or *subtonic*) scale degree.

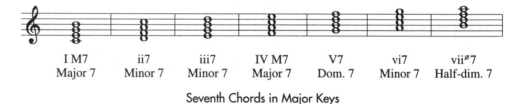

I M7	ii7	iii7	IV M7	V7	vi7	vii⌀7
Major 7	Minor 7	Minor 7	Major 7	Dom. 7	Minor 7	Half-dim. 7

Seventh Chords in Major Keys

Seventh Chords in Minor Keys

Exercise 4

Given the key and the chord, write the appropriate roman numeral below each chord. (Be sure to differentiate between uppercase and lowercase numerals, and use "M" and "⌀" to denote major and diminished qualities.) The first two are done for you.

A♭: __V7__   c: __VI M7__   D:_____   f♯:_____   B:_____

Eb: _____   g: _____   E: _____   bb: _____   Db: _____

CHORD INVERSIONS AND VOICINGS

When a chord is built in 3rds with the root on the bottom, it is referred to as a *root-position* chord. It is also possible to write chords so that the 3rd, the 5th, or the 7th is on the bottom. These are called *chord inversions*. When the 3rd is the lowest note, the chord is said to be in *first inversion;* when the 5th is on the bottom, the chord is in *second inversion;* when the 7th is the lowest note, the chord is in *third inversion.*

Root Position   First Inversion   Second Inversion   Third Inversion

If the top and bottom notes in a chord are within one octave, the chord is in *close position.* When the chord spans more than an octave, it is in *open position.* This is often accomplished by dropping the second or third highest notes down an octave (known as *drop-2* and *drop-3 voicings*).

Close Position   Open Position, Drop-2   Open Position, Drop-3

Adding chord extensions beyond the 7th and experimenting with different ways of stacking the notes make many other voicings possible. Nonessential notes, such as the 5th or the root, may be left out of the voicing, assuming a bass player is present. The 3rd and the 7th, however, are typically present in most chord voicings.

Exercise 5

Write the following chords in close position, using the indicated inversions.

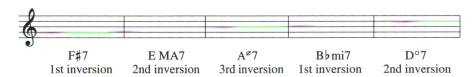

F#7   E MA7   A⌀7   Bbmi7   D°7
1st inversion   2nd inversion   3rd inversion   1st inversion   2nd inversion

Exercise 6

Create open-position voicings by changing the following example as indicated.

Close position   Drop-2   Drop-3

CHORD PROGRESSIONS

Chords do not occur in a random order; they progress in a way that sounds pleasing to the ear. Strong chord progressions set up an expectation of resolution and finality, whereas weak chord progressions create a feeling of vagueness and movement away from the key center. Strong progressions consist of root movements down a perfect 5th or up a perfect 4th; weak progressions tend to move by 3rds or 6ths. A diatonic chord progression in which each chord moves down a perfect 5th would look like this:

C: iii7   vi7   ii7   V7   I M7

The iii–vi–ii–V–I Progression

This progression includes all the diatonic chords found in a major key except the vii°7 chord, which is usually used as a *substitute* for the V7 chord, and the IV chord, which is a substitute for the ii chord. A similar progression in a minor key would look like this:

C: III M7   VI M7   ii°7   V7   i7

The III–VI–ii–V–i Progression

The iii–vi–ii–V–I progression can be varied through the use of *secondary dominants*. Normally, only one dominant 7th chord occurs in any key—the V7 chord. However, it is possible to change the iii, vi, and ii chords from minor 7th to dominant 7th chords by raising the 3rd of each chord a half step. The resulting chords are called secondary dominants because they create a dominant-to-tonic relationship to a chord other than the tonic. Since they act as a V7 to the vi, ii, and V chords, they are labeled V7/vi, V7/ii, and V7/V (pronounced V7 of vi, V7 of ii, and V7 of V).

C: V7/vi   V7/ii   V7/V   V7   I M7

The V7/vi–V7/ii–V7/V–V7–I Progression

Chord progressions can also be modified through the use of the *tritone substitution*. For any dominant 7th chord, you can substitute the dominant 7th chord a tritone (or an augmented 4th/diminished 5th) away. This is possible because the essential members of the chord (the 3rds and the 7ths) are enharmonically interchangeable.

The iii–vi–ii–V–I progression (or some variation utilizing secondary dominants and tritone substitutions) occurs in countless numbers of standard songs. Mastering this progression will greatly simplify the process of learning standard repertoire.

Some jazz compositions, particularly those written after 1960, intentionally avoided using these standard chord progressions. Composers from that period were looking for new sounds and often used weak chord movements and drew on chords that were not diatonic to the key. This type of harmony is referred to as *nonfunctional* because the chords cannot be analyzed as functioning within a particular key. *Modal harmony*, in which the chords last four measures or longer, also became commonplace during this period.

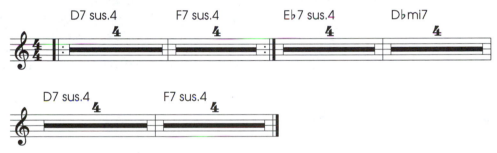

Chord Progression to Herbie Hancock's "Maiden Voyage"[1]

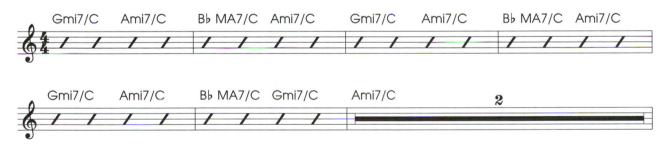

Chord Progression to the First Phrase of Miles Davis's "Milestones"[2]

[1]Herbie Hancock, "Maiden Voyage" (copyright 1973 by Hancock Music, New York).
[2]Miles Davis, "Milestones" (copyright 1947, renewed 1975 Screen Gems–EMI Music).

Exercise 7

Write the chord symbols indicated by the roman numerals.

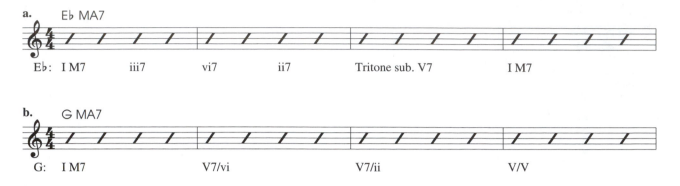

a. Eb MA7

Eb: I M7   iii7   vi7   ii7   Tritone sub. V7   I M7

b. G MA7

G: I M7   V7/vi   V7/ii   V/V

Voice Leading

When chord progressions are written or played, the chord tones should move by a step or a 3rd to the closest note in the following chord. This is known as smooth *voice leading.* In progressions of 7th chords with root movements of 4ths and 5ths, the 3rd of the first chord typically becomes the 7th of the following chord, and vice versa. The remaining chord tones move to the closest available note, creating chord inversions. Compare these two examples of iii–vi–ii–V–I progressions:

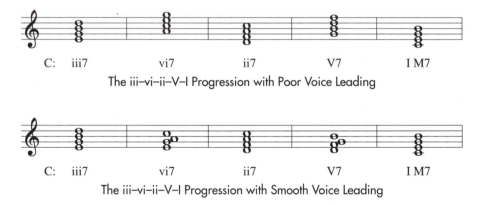

C: iii7   vi7   ii7   V7   I M7

The iii–vi–ii–V–I Progression with Poor Voice Leading

C: iii7   vi7   ii7   V7   I M7

The iii–vi–ii–V–I Progression with Smooth Voice Leading

Exercise 8

Write the chords indicated by the roman numerals, using principles of good voice leading.

G: iii7   vi7   ii7   V7   I M7

The Relationship of Scales and Modes to Chords

As previously mentioned, for every chord there is at least one scale that best colors it. The previous chapters in this text and those in *Creative Jazz Improvisation* will reinforce your knowledge of these relationships and develop your ability to improvise on them.[3] The following is a summary of most of the chords used in jazz and the scales that color them.

Chord Type	Scales or Modes
1. Major 7	Major, Lydian, Major pentatonic
2. Major 7 ♯11 or Major 7 ♭5	Lydian, Lydian augmented, Major pentatonic (a major 2nd above the root of the chord)
3. Major 7 ♯5	Lydian augmented
4. Unaltered dominant 9	Mixolydian, Bebop 7th, Major pentatonic
5. Dominant 7♯9 or Dominant 7♭9	Diminished (half-step), Superlocrian, Blues
6. Dominant 9♯5	Whole-tone
7. Dominant 9♭5	Whole-tone, Lydian dominant
8. Dominant 7♯9♭5 or Dominant 7♭9♭5	Diminished (half-step), Superlocrian
9. Dominant 7♯9♯5 or Dominant 7♭9♯5	Superlocrian
10. Minor 7	Dorian, Aeolian, Phrygian, Minor pentatonic, Blues
11. Minor/major 7	Harmonic Minor, Melodic Minor
12. Half-diminished 7	Locrian, locrian ♯2
13. Fully diminished 7	Diminished (whole-step)

Exercise 9

Next to the following chords, write the name and the notes of the scales that best color them. In some cases, there may be more than one right answer. One is done for you as an example.

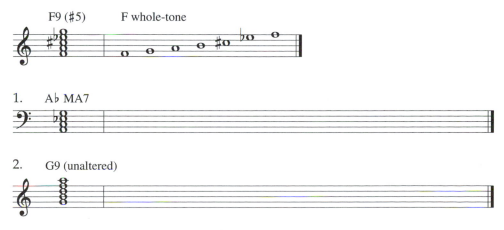

---

[3]Scott D. Reeves, *Creative Jazz Improvisation*, 2nd ed. (Englewood Cliffs, N.J.: Prentice Hall, 1995).

3.   Bmi7

4.   Emi (MA7)

5.   D⌀7

6.   C7(♯9,♭5)

7.   F♯°7

8.   F MA7(♭5)

Jazz Forms

Besides knowing the melody and the chords of a song, an improvisor must have an instinctive grasp of the form. Except for free-form styles, most jazz compositions are based on either *blues* or *sectional forms.*

The blues form has its origins in the traditional call-and-response practices found in African music. This procedure was carried over into other early African-American musical styles, such as work songs, church music, and blues.

It should be pointed out that the *blues form* is not always identical with a "blues feeling." In fact, jazz compositions based on the blues form can be uplifting, mysterious, or complex in nature. The blues form is not exclusive to the musical style called *the blues* and is found in jazz, rock 'n' roll, boogie-woogie, and other popular styles.

Typically, the blues form is 12 measures long and consists of three 4-bar phrases. In its simplest format, these three phrases form a question-question-answer format. In more complex blues compositions, this call-and-response procedure is not as evident.

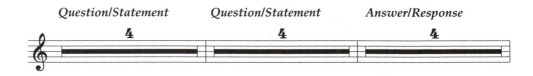

Question/Statement   *Question/Statement*   *Answer/Response*

The chord progression to a basic blues in the key of C would be as follows:

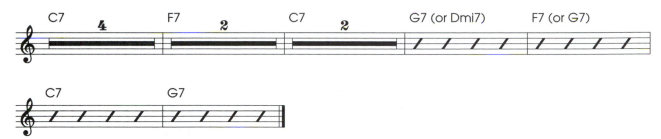

There are many variations on this basic progression, including complex formulas that utilize additional chords and substitutions. For a more thorough discussion of these variations, refer to Chapter 9 of *Creative Jazz Improvisation*.[4]

Sectional forms have phrases that occur in a given sequence, typically four phrases of 8 measures each, resulting in a 32-measure form. Sometimes we find a sectional form in which the phrases are 4 bars long, resulting in a 16-bar form. Irregular phrase lengths and other variations of this format also occasionally occur. In the analysis of the phrases of a song, letters are assigned to each new phrase.

Depending on the order of the phrases, sectional forms occur in three types: *binary form,* in which the song appears to be divided in half and the phrases occur in an AB-AB or AB-AC format; *ternary form,* in which the song is divided into thirds and the phrases occur in an AA-B-A format; and *through-composed form,* in which none of the phrases repeats.

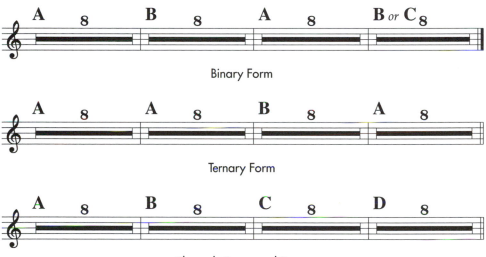

As you play or listen to music, be continually aware of the form of the song. Inwardly singing the melody while listening to other musicians improvise may aid in developing this awareness.

E x e r c i s e   1 0

Listen to recorded improvisations and identify the form of the song. See if you can keep your place during drum solos over the form.

[4]Reeves, *Creative Jazz Improvisation*, p. 102.

It's up to all of us to make sure that arts and music education in the schools doesn't disappear. We have to start demanding it again—that it be part of everyone's education. A society—a world—without art is doomed as far as I'm concerned. . . . As long as there are musicians who have a passion for spontaneity, for creating something that's never been done before, the art form of jazz will flourish.

—bassist Charlie Haden

INDEX